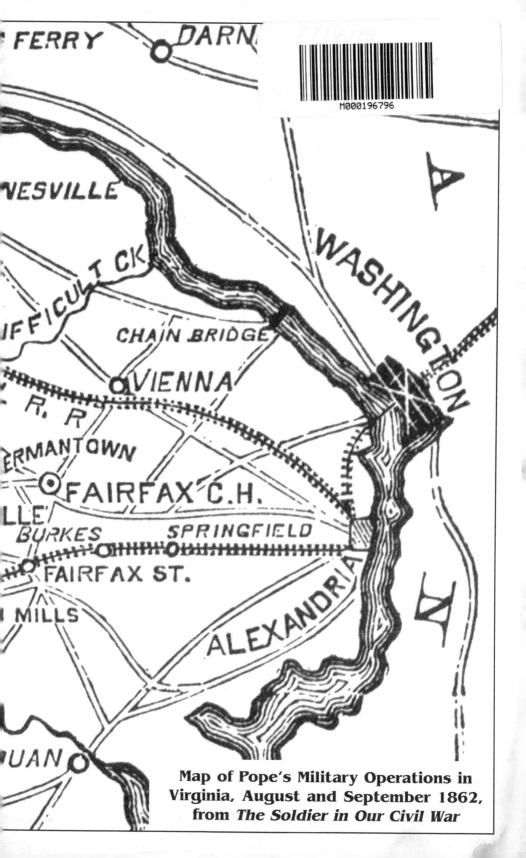

FERRY

DARN

NESVILLE

IFFICULT CK

IFFICUL T CK

CHAIN BRIDGE

VIENNA

RR

ERMANTOWN

FAIRFAX C.H.

LLE

BURKES

SPRINGFIELD

FAIRFAX ST.

MILLS

UAN

WASHINGTON

ALEXANDRIA

Map of Pope's Military Operations in Virginia, August and September 1862, from *The Soldier in Our Civil War*

He Hath Loosed
the
Fateful Lightning

The Battle of Ox Hill (Chantilly), September 1, 1862

Paul Taylor

WHITE MANE BOOKS
SHIPPENSBURG, PENNSYLVANIA

Maps were prepared by the author and drawn by Jim Robinson.

This White Mane Books publication
was printed by
Beidel Printing House, Inc.
63 West Burd Street
Shippensburg, PA 17257-0708 USA

The acid-free paper used in this book meets the guidelines for permanence and durability of the Committee on Production Guidelines for Book Longevity of the Council on Library Resources.

For a complete list of available publications
please write
White Mane Books
Division of White Mane Publishing Company, Inc.
P.O. Box 708
Shippensburg, PA 17257-0708 USA

Library of Congress Cataloging-in-Publication Data

Taylor, Paul, 1959-
    He hath loosed the fateful lightning : the Battle of Ox Hill (Chantilly), September 1, 1862
/ Paul Taylor.
        p. cm.
    Includes bibliographical references and index.
    ISBN 1-57249-329-1 (acid-free paper)
    1. Chantilly, Battle of, Va., 1862. 2. Chantilly, Battle of, Va., 1862--Personal narratives.
I. Title.

E473.77.T39 2003
973.7'33--dc21

2002044918

PRINTED IN THE UNITED STATES OF AMERICA

*Mine eyes have seen the glory of the coming of
the Lord
He is trampling out the vintage where the grapes
of wrath are stored,
He hath loosed the fateful lightning of His terrible
swift sword
His truth is marching on!*
—The Battle Hymn of the Republic

*And the courage of the man who braved death
in the darkness at Chantilly, let no man question*
—Clara Barton

A considerable little fight was fought this evening
—Dr. James Boulware, Asst. Surgeon,
6th South Carolina, writing in his diary the
night of September 1, 1862

"Dulce et decorum est pro patria mori"

CONTENTS

List of Illustrations vi

List of Maps viii

Acknowledgments ix

Chapter 1—*"Disaster and shame are in the retreat"*—The Arrival of John Pope and the Second Manassas Campaign 1

Chapter 2—*"I suppose I've captured the dinner also!"*—Opening Movements—August 31, 1862 17

Chapter 3—*"I think we will have a fight before night"*—Early Morning to Mid-Afternoon—September 1, 1862 36

Chapter 4—*"That hat will be the death of him"*—Late Afternoon and Early Evening—September 1, 1862 47

Chapter 5—*"The upturned faces of the dead"*—Late Evening, September 1 to Early Morning, September 2 92

Chapter 6—*"A beastly, comfortless conflict"*—Medical and Casualty Situation in the Aftermath 100

Chapter 7—*"None of us seemed anxious"*—Afterward and the Days to Follow 109

Epilogue—The Battlefield Area Today 125

Appendix 1—Union General Isaac Ingalls Stevens 130

Appendix 2—Union General Philip Kearny 132

Appendix 3—The Kearny Patch and Medal 134

Appendix 4—Order of Battle at Ox Hill 136

Notes 143

Bibliography 160

Index 176

ILLUSTRATIONS

General John Pope 4
Federal baggage train of Pope's army 10
Jackson's troops pillaging 12
March of Longstreet's corps through Thoroughfare Gap 14
The retreat over the stone bridge, Saturday evening,
    August 30 15
View of the fortifications on Centreville heights 19
Between the lines during a truce.. 21
General Ambrose Powell Hill.. 23
The Ayre stone house 25
General "Jeb" Stuart, Confederate cavalry 29
Supper after a hard march 34
Sketch of General Thomas J. "Stonewall" Jackson 39
General Jesse L. Reno 47
Fatigue uniform and kilts of the 79th New York 49
Colonel Edward Ferrero 51
Colonel John M. Brockenbrough.. 53
General Lawrence O'Bryan Branch 53
Early 1900s view of the Chantilly battlefield............................ 57
Confederate line in the woods 60
General Isaac Ingalls Stevens 61
Colonel Henry B. Strong 64
Captain William F. Brown, 12th Georgia Infantry 65
General William E. Starke 67
General Jubal Early—an 1850s image 68
General Edward L. Thomas 71

General Maxcy Gregg 71
The extant woods on the eastside of the battlefield 73
General Philip Kearny 79
General Alexander R. Lawton 80
General David B. Birney 82
Death of General Kearny 85
General James Longstreet 90
General Orlando M. Poe 97
General John Robinson 98
Modern view of St. Mary's Church 103
General William Dorsey Pender 110
Modern view of the original Fairfax Court House 116
Jedediah Hotchkiss, Stonewall Jackson's cartographer 117
John N. Ballard as a young man during the war 127
Early twentieth-century view of the Kearny-Stevens
    monuments 129
Modern view of the Kearny-Stevens monuments 129

MAPS

Area of Operations—Fairfax County 28

Morning, September 1 37

Late Afternoon, September 1 50

Confederate Line 55

5:00 P.M.—Phase 1: Stevens Attacks 62

Confederate Line Briefly Breaks 66

6:00 P.M.—Phase 2: Birney Attacks 81

2:00 A.M.—September 2 96

ACKNOWLEDGMENTS

Though only one name usually appears as author on a book's cover, the belief that many assisted with and contributed to the final product is a truism that shows itself as fact time and again. This work is certainly no exception.

Much of the research for this book was conducted at the Virginia Room of the Fairfax County Public Library, Fairfax, Virginia. Brian Conley and staff were always pleasant and helpful, and I heartily thank them for their gracious efforts. In addition, living so close to Washington, D.C., afforded me the opportunity to access in person the wonderful collections of the Library of Congress. Special appreciation goes out to the Library's professional staff, who never failed to offer insightful tips about researching within the various Reading Rooms. Numerous other repositories of manuscript material were within a reasonable drive, and I would like to recognize their first-rate collections and kind personal assistance: Dr. Richard Sommers and his staff at the United States Army Military History Institute in Carlisle, Pennsylvania; Jim Burgess and Terri Bard at the Manassas National Battlefield Park Library; Mr. Gregory Stoner at the Virginia Historical Society; Mr. John Coski of the Eleanor Brockenbrough Library, Museum of the Confederacy, Richmond, Virginia; the staff at the Library of Virginia, Richmond, Virginia; John Craft at the Civil War Library and Museum, Philadelphia, Pennsylvania. Any student of this battle must also acknowledge Mr. Mario Espinola, whose decades-long archeological study of the battlefield has brought about much-needed public awareness to Ox Hill (Chantilly).

Other institutions and individuals provided answers to my many questions and offered sound advice through traditional and electronic mail. They were: Ms. Karen Jania of the Bentley Historical Library, University of Michigan; Mr. Neal Crochetiere, Reference Librarian at the Rockland Public Library, Rockland, Maine; Ms. Kate DuBose of the Massachusetts Historical Society; Ms. Sharon Steinberg of the Connecticut Historical Society; Mr. David Smolen of the New Hampshire Historical Society; Ms. Elizabeth Shoemaker of Emory University; the staff at the New York State Archives; and the staff at the Historical Society of Montgomery County, Pennsylvania.

The hunt for photographs of the battle's participants sometimes proved challenging. I would like to thank Mr. Don Clay of Elkton, Maryland, who helped me locate the post-war image of Colonel John Brockenbrough. If anyone has, or knows of an image of the colonel taken during the war, please let Don and me know! I would also like to thank Ms. Diane Jacob, Archivist at the Virginia Military Institute, who provided the photograph of a younger Jubal Early, as well as the Valentine Museum in Richmond, Virginia, for permission to use their Jeb Stuart photograph. Thanks also go out to Mr. John Kuhl of Pittstown, New Jersey, for permission to use his Philip Kearny carte-de-visite. Brian Conley at the Fairfax County Library alerted me to the early twentieth-century newspaper photo of a young John Ballard. Thanks again, Brian! A big tip of the hat goes to Mr. James Gannon, author of *Irish Rebels, Confederate Tigers: A History of the 6th Louisiana Volunteers,* for his input regarding the image of Colonel Henry Strong. Sadly, we have both concluded that this poor, though discernible, image of the colonel is the only one in existence. We would both be delighted to be proven wrong.

Different types of support were rendered closer to the end of the road. I would like to thank my friend, Fiona Candlish, as well as Mr. Henry E. Howard for various copyediting suggestions to the rough manuscript. Once the final manuscript was submitted, Mr. Harold Collier, Marianne Zinn, and Vicki Stouffer of White Mane Publishing offered invaluable guidance and patience. My heartfelt thanks to all of you.

Lastly, and certainly not least, the greatest thanks of all goes out to my loving wife, Miriam, whose patience and understanding with this book knew no bounds.

"Disaster and shame are in the retreat" 1

The Arrival of John Pope and the Second Manassas Campaign

The September 1, 1862, Civil War battle at Ox Hill, Virginia, fought near the once magnificent plantation estate, neighboring post office, and surrounding area that all bore the name of Chantilly, marked the final engagement in what has become known as the Union Army of Virginia's Northern Virginia Campaign of 1862. It followed by two days the battle of Second Manassas, or Second Bull Run as it was called in the North, which was the largest battle of the campaign and ultimately one of the largest battles of the Civil War. The fact that it followed so closely on the heels of the huge engagement at Manassas, and then became quickly usurped in discussions both north and south by Robert E. Lee's first invasion of Maryland, has contributed to many historians' relegating Ox Hill to little more than rear-guard status, a mere skirmish in the broad course of the war, but its outcome helped prompt significant change to the strategic plans of both camps.

Two other important factors helped add to the relative historical obscurity of this engagement. Though obviously unconscious of its historical effects at the time, Union General in Chief Henry Halleck's order from Washington of August 19, 1862, stipulated to Union commanding general John Pope that "You will immediately remove from your army all newspaper reporters, and you will permit no telegrams to be sent over the telegraph wires out of your command except those sent by yourself. You will also suspend the transmission of any mail matter other than that of official communication."

This type of journalistic censorship had heretofore never existed, and was prompted by Halleck's belief that Pope's staffers were leaking operational details immediately once decided upon with journalists who were in camp. Unsure at that point whether he would actually act on the matter, a day later Pope acted on this decree when he was again advised by Halleck that "The substance of my telegrams to you is immediately telegraphed back here to the press. Several of these telegrams have been intercepted. Clean out all such characters from your headquarters. It is useless to attempt any sending of orders if you permit them to be made public as soon as you receive them."[1]

Pope's level of enforcement of this order and its subsequent effect on the number of journalists present during the campaign are unclear. Some sources claimed that only two Northern reporters were actually present at the Second Bull Run battle. In any event, virtually no news of note could be gathered by readers of Northern papers during the final days of the campaign. The Washington, D.C., correspondent of the *New York Commercial Advertiser* wrote on August 25, 1862, "Nothing relating to either the enemy or our forces is allowed to pass the censorship at the present time. This is the most strict rule put in force since the war began." Mail from soldiers to their loved ones back home was also eliminated for fear of camp and operational details being discovered by the enemy. A New Hampshire soldier's letter written after the campaign ended typified the average private's sentiment: "After a long time, the col. informs us that we can send letters home, and I hasten to improve the opportunity. Pages might be written upon what has passed during the past three weeks."[2]

As such, the lack of mail delivery and of newspaper reporters present in the Union camp from late August to early September 1862, as compared to previous campaigns, resulted in the battles of Second Manassas and Ox Hill receiving relatively scant attention in the national media at the time. These strange circumstances were soon forgotten, like the fierce battle of Ox Hill itself, once Lee's first Northern invasion was under way in early September.[3]

In addition, a significant number of field-grade officers, both blue and gray, would be dead by the time their official battle reports would normally have been written. Three important Union generals, three Confederate generals, two Confederate colonels, and one captain, all of whom commanded divisions or brigades at Ox Hill, would either lose their lives or be seriously wounded during that fight, or sometime during the following two and-one-half-week

Maryland Campaign. The lack of written record that they would have certainly contributed has also been sorely missed by Civil War scholars.[4] The written record of Ox Hill that was left by many surviving officers could also be considered miniscule, at best. The most striking example is the official report by John Pope, the Union's commanding major general. He gave the battle at Ox Hill all of three sentences, though his full report of the entire northern Virginia campaign takes up six pages within the *Official Records*. In 1998, Pope's long-lost military memoirs were republished. The Ox Hill fight is not even mentioned.

Given that the battle at Ox Hill was fought at a corps level, with Thomas J. "Stonewall" Jackson's entire wing spread out in a line of battle over one-half mile long, and with two Union divisions actively engaged, this fight deserves a more prominent spot in the annals of the Civil War.

The initial engagement of the Union campaign was at the battle of Cedar Mountain on August 9, 1862, but the operation had its roots with the arrival on June 26 of John Pope as its new commander. With three scattered Federal forces under Generals Irvin McDowell, Nathaniel Banks, and John Fremont unable to silence Stonewall Jackson in the Shenandoah Valley, these armies were consolidated in the summer of 1862 into the newly created Union Army of Virginia, with Major General John Pope in command. An 1842 West Point graduate, the forty-year-old Pope was considered a very capable military man who had achieved significant success in the Western theater at the battles of New Madrid and Island Number 10. Though Pope pointed out to President Abraham Lincoln that each of the three generals he was now commanding was his senior in rank, Lincoln was adamant. Pope's offensive-minded tactics were the breath of fresh air that Lincoln had been looking for in a field general, in light of the maddening caution that he felt his past and current commanders displayed. Lincoln's executive order of June 26 clearly laid out the mission of the new command. In addition to protecting the capital, they were to "threaten the enemy in the direction of Charlottesville, and render the most effective aid to relieve General McClellan and capture Richmond."[5]

Unfortunately, John Pope was also considered a braggart by many who knew him, and had the habit of rubbing those around him

General John Pope

the wrong way. His braggadocio got him off to a very poor start with his new men when he boasted on July 14, 1862, that the Western armies from whence he had come were "used to seeing the backs of our enemy...whose policy has been attack and not defense" and that their methods had been "to find, attack and defeat the enemy...Success and glory are in the advance, disaster and shame lurk in the rear."[6] Many Eastern soldiers took his statements as a backhanded slap at their less-than-stellar results against Robert E. Lee's Confederate Army of Northern Virginia. Upon his arrival in Washington, Pope, it is said, had declared that his headquarters would be in the saddle, prompting some soldiers to proclaim derisively that his hindquarters should be where his headquarters were.

Part of his initial orders dealt with the civilian population of northern Virginia and especially those suspected of secessionist leanings. His tactics were rough and highly controversial for the day; he ordered (General Orders No. 5) that Union officers had the authority to seize provisions for their troops from the Virginia citizenry, with vouchers to be given to the owners payable at the end of the war, provided that such citizens had been loyal citizens since the date of the voucher. The ire of civilians was raised to the extreme with Pope's General Orders No. 7, which stated that any civilian living within five miles of damage perpetrated to Union supply lines or soldiers by rebel guerrillas was to be turned out to the damage to repair it themselves, and their property confiscated to pay for the expense.

Those civilians caught in the act of guerrilla activity, or possibly even suspected, would be shot immediately without civil process. On July 23, 1862, Pope ordered that all civilian males within Federal lines who refused to pledge loyalty to the Union were to be escorted south beyond the furthermost pickets of the Union line, and left there with the warning that if caught in the future within Union lines they would be considered spies and summarily shot. The local pro-Southern citizenry was aghast at this heretofore unheard of treatment of their property, as evidenced by one local who vented his wrath: "Of all the things in the world that I hate it is fighting, but it would afford me the greatest pleasure to thrash that contemptible scoundrel, but we will pay him up for it yet."[7]

Confederate authorities rightly believed in the early spring of 1862 that Union forces would attempt some type of move on Richmond, so those rebel troops stationed in Fairfax County, Virginia, were withdrawn to new positions south of the Rappahannock River in order to defend the Southern capital. This evacuation of the area prompted Federal authorities to begin trying to set up some facsimile of a "loyal" civilian government in northern Virginia. By April, a civilian government that existed more on paper than in practice was in place, and a semblance of normalcy returned. Resident emotions on both sides ran deep as both Union and Confederate sympathizers often found themselves as neighbors and therefore at odds with each other. Scores of soldiers in the area and shortages of food and wood for fuel added to an often tense scenario, with Southern citizens often on the short end of the stick due to Pope's approved foraging from Union soldiers.

This harsh treatment of Southern civilians did not escape the stern wrath and notice of Robert E. Lee either, as history would record that John Pope was the only Union commander who, in facing Lee, managed to earn the Confederate general's personal disdain. Lee contemptuously referred to Pope as a miscreant, in consideration of his draconian treatment and tactics against the civilian population.[8] The Confederate general also fired off a stern letter of protest to Union General George McClellan whose Army of the Potomac was battling the Confederates on the Virginia peninsula east of Richmond. Lee refused to acknowledge the legitimacy of Pope's orders regarding the extraction of loyalty oaths from the Southern populace and warned McClellan that any measures of punishment against civilians meted out by Union authorities would be met with appropriate retaliatory measures.[9] Though hard-handed and certainly controversial with Northerners and Southerners alike, John Pope realized two years before William Sherman's march to the sea that a "total warfare" concept would be needed to subdue the enemy.

Slaughter Mountain

Pope immediately sought the initiative and in early August ordered his army southward along the Orange and Alexandria Railroad, with the goal of severing the line farther south at Gordonsville. The overall Union strategy was that by converging on the railroad, the Confederate government in Richmond would be compelled to siphon off troops from the capital to cover their northern flank. This would then allow McClellan to resume his stalled Peninsula campaign. However, just days before, Lee learned of the Federal advance and had promptly sent Stonewall Jackson north to Gordonsville "to meet the advance of the enemy [Pope] and restrain, as far as possible, the atrocities which he threatened to perpetrate upon our defenseless citizens." His orders to Stonewall were clear: "I want Pope to be suppressed."[10]

Union divisions under Generals Samuel W. Crawford and Nathaniel Banks were the first to enter the small village of Culpeper, though they were unaware that Stonewall Jackson, having now been joined by the Light Division of General Ambrose Powell Hill, was bringing his army of 24,000 north from Gordonsville to stop their advance. Jackson's men had earned the complimentary sobriquet "foot cavalry" due to their lightning quick marches during the spring's romp through the Shenandoah Valley, but speed and dexterity were not forthcoming now. Jackson repeatedly complained of the slow progress of Hill's troops, but Hill had barely even moved due to a miscommunication of orders. Jackson later advised Lee that Hill's division was too large for proper maneuvering and then solved the matter by taking a brigade away from Hill. This set the stage for a celebrated row between the two Confederate generals that would last for months, to the consternation of Robert E. Lee. In fact, Lee had feared just such a clash between the proud Hill and secretive Jackson, diplomatically urging Stonewall in a letter of July 27 that he would find Hill "a good officer with whom you can consult and by advising with your division commanders as to your movements much trouble will be saved you...."[11]

While his Federal adversaries were blind to the size of his force, Jackson was likewise unaware that Union troops had already arrived in Culpeper. The enigmatic Jackson had planned to reach there by the morning of August 8 to engage the various scattered commands, but one delay after another prevented his arrival until the ninth. On August 9, the two armies brawled about six miles south of Culpeper beneath a rise known as Cedar Mountain by some, Slaughter Mountain by others, that was bordered by a narrow stream known as Cedar Run.

The battle began in earnest as an artillery duel. Confederate cavalry had brought word to Jackson that Union troops and cannon were arriving in force below the mountain. Jackson countered by sending his guns ahead to seek out the most advantageous positions from which to shell their foe. The rebel guns were posted to the right of the road along the edge of Cedar Mountain as well as on a small hill off to the left. Here, an artillery duel that was later termed by one rebel as "the prettiest artillery duel ever witnessed during the war" was waged for about an hour between Union and Confederate gunners. Confederate losses during the shelling were then magnified when much-respected General Charles S. Winder was mortally wounded by a shell fragment while directing the fire of his guns. The slow yearlong deterioration of quality Confederate field commanders had continued.[12]

Under cover of the artillery duel and despite orders from Pope to the contrary, General Nathaniel Banks had sent his Union troops advancing through the thick woods on the Confederate far left and broke through the thin infantry defense. As Jackson frantically rode forward, he was greeted by his own men running pell-mell away from the furious Yankee assault. Realizing that the left of their line was breaking, many simply dropped their muskets and ran from the storm of lead. Jackson was mortified at the sight of his soldiers breaking in disorder, and for the only recorded time in the war drew his sword and urged his men to rally behind him, crying out, "Rally, brave men, and press forward! Your general will lead you. Jackson will lead you. Follow me!"[13]

He found an aide and urgently ordered, "Tell Hill to bring his men up at once." Lawrence Branch's brigade, as well as James Archer's and William Dorsey Pender's arrived in the nick of time, counterattacking on the left against the weary Federal forces. These fresh troops helped to stall the Yankee advance. Archer's and Pender's brigades launched a charge through a wheatfield that sent the Union troops retreating.[14] Stonewall's beleaguered Confederates also could see help through the smoke off to their far right. "We could plainly see Ewell, with a part of his division on Slaughter Mountain, way off to the right of our line, advancing too; as the mountain at this point was free of woods, we could see his skirmish line in front advancing down the mountain, his line of battle following, and his cannon belching forth fire and smoke, and we could see the enemy's shell bursting on the mountain side. It was a magnificent and inspiring sight."[15] The tide turned, and what could have easily been a Confederate rout was turned into a victory.

The next morning Pope requested a truce from Jackson so that his troops could retrieve their wounded and dead from the field. Jackson readily agreed, as he had his share of slain to deal with. James Orr of the 37th Virginia was put in charge of a burial detail at Cedar Mountain and remembered that "We had no coffins, nothing but tools to dig with. We dug graves about seven feet square, and laid the dead soldiers, wrapped in their blankets, in these graves and covered them with earth, not knowing who they were, and had no means of marking their graves."[16] Jackson also had an ulterior motive in quickly acquiescing to Pope's request: the delay gave him time to withdraw his bloodied brigades across the Rapidan and Robinson Rivers, near the spot from which he had originally marched.

The next several days saw brief skirmishing and scarce provisions for rebel stomachs. Many men survived solely on green corn and apples. Yet morale was high, for "Old Jack" had brought his men another triumph. Like his ragged legions, Stonewall certainly had none of the spit and polish that so many of his Union counterparts aspired to. Upon seeing him in person for the first time following the battle of Cedar Mountain, Private William Snakenberg of the 14th Louisiana witnessed Jackson being cheered by the men he passed. Snakenberg saw "a very ordinary looking person, riding a small sorrel horse, like a house on fire, along the road, about 100 yards off, who looked like a Jew peddlar [sic]. He had on an old, faded, long-tail coat and a military cap with the peak pulled down over his eyes and set stooped forward in the saddle."[17]

Pope's army did not bother to pursue once the truce was over. Instead they withdrew north of the Rappahannock River. The first battle on the road to Ox Hill was over.

By mid-August, George McClellan's Union Army of the Potomac was still camped on the Virginia Peninsula and had been stalled there for days on end. A change in plan was called for, so it was ordered back to Washington to consolidate with Pope's army in northern Virginia, which was still sitting on the Rappahannock River. Once united, the combined forces could then advance on the Confederate capital of Richmond in overwhelming numbers. When McClellan began moving north Lee immediately surmised the Federal intent, and on August 25, 1862, Lee ordered Confederate General Stonewall Jackson and his 24,000 men to march on a northwest trek

**Federal baggage train of Pope's army making
its way towards Manassas Junction**

The Soldier in Our Civil War

through the Bull Run mountains, keeping out of Pope's front, but then swing back through Thoroughfare Gap to come up on Pope's rear. Pope mistakenly believed this was a mere feint, essentially did nothing, and then realized the stark, eyeopening truth of Jackson's stealth movement on the 26th. Stonewall had marched his men with the utmost celerity and concealment, knowing that they were near their enemy. The men's knapsacks had been dropped off at a large warehouse in Stevensburg to ensure a light, fast march was obtained. In addition, orders had been sent down the line not to talk above a whisper and to make sure that their canteens did not rattle.[18] Late on August 26, Jackson's men swooped down on the railroad at Bristoe Station, tearing up the tracks and capturing three trains of supplies.[19] Stonewall then went on to attack the Federal supply depot at Manassas where the always underfed and hungry rebels feasted on mountains of Union rations, including such delicacies as "potted ham, lobster, tongue, candy, cakes, nuts, oranges, lemons, etc.". The scene was one of "general jubilee." "Fine cigars circulated freely, elegant lawn and linen handkerchiefs were applied to noses hitherto blown with thumb and forefinger and sumptuous underclothing was fitted over limbs sunburnt, sore and vermin splotched." Important provisions such as salt, clothing, and wagons were also secured.[20]

Whiskey and brandy were other provisions that the soldiers always sought, and they were on hand in abundant quantities at the junction, but Stonewall, wanting to ensure his battle-hardened veterans would stay that way, made certain they would taste none of it. He ordered several of his most trusted officers to knock the heads out of the numerous kegs that were discovered, spilling the liquor all to the ground. "I fear that whiskey more than I do General Pope's whole army" was the pious general's justification.[21] In spite of his best efforts, some of the drink found its way into rebel canteens. James Orr smilingly recollected: "Lieutenant William Miller and myself filled our canteens half full of brandy and then poured in strawberry syrup and had a delicious drink."[22] With their stomachs and thirsts satiated, the Confederates refitted their military accoutrements before destroying and firing what could not be carried off. When the fires got to the ammunition trains, the explosions and racket created rivaled that of the loudest battle.[23] Union troops arriving after the fact were dismayed at the destruction left by the rebels. Sergeant Elisha Bracken of the 100th Pennsylvania noted in his diary that "...two long trains of cars were still burning. It was a sad sight to see the dreadful destruction of property but sadder still was it to cast our eyes to the left and see the dead bodies of both friends and enemies killed in the fight yesterday and still unburied."[24]

Lee and Jackson both knew what the growing Federal menace would entail if Pope and McClellan successfully united. They realized that a decisive battle would have to be fought before the Federal armies could combine. The Southern generals recognized they had to draw Pope out. Jackson's men marched on August 28 from the smoldering wreckage at Manassas Junction to a wooded ridge on the northwestern edge of the first Bull Run battlefield, near the small village of Groveton, with the intent of simply staying hidden. Pope assumed Jackson was still at Manassas and intended to

**Jackson's troops pillaging the Union
depot of supplies at Manassas Junction**

Battles and Leaders

engage him. In typical Pope style, he ordered General Irvin McDowell's Third Corps to march to Manassas Junction and declaring that "if you march promptly and rapidly, at the earliest dawn of day, we shall bag the whole crowd."[25] When the army arrived, Jackson was obviously gone, the assumption being that he had fled westward back through the mountains.

While the Federal army division of Rufus King was wearily trudging eastward on the Warrenton Turnpike *(modern Route 29)* late in the afternoon of August 28, Jackson's Confederates attacked from the woods. For several hours both sides hammered away at each other, often standing within a stone's throw of their foe, neither side attacking nor retreating, the net result being several thousand casualties. Pope now knew where Jackson was, and Jackson had succeeded in drawing Pope out without McClellan, setting the stage for a large-scale fight the next day. August 29 dawned with Jackson's men ensconced in an unfinished railroad bed cut along the northern edge of the old battlefield. His left wing stopped at the village of Sudley Springs, right next to Bull Run while his right ended at the

Brawner farm west of Groveton. Pope had Jackson firmly in his sights, yet the full coordinated attack on the 29th never materialized. Instead, only a series of relatively small, uncoordinated attacks occurred. Three times throughout the day, Union forces probed the rebel line, first the center, then the left, then back to the center. Each attack was able to briefly penetrate Jackson's line, but as no support was forthcoming, Pope gave Jackson the needed opportunity to fill the line each time with reinforcements and repulse the Union attackers.

Throughout the day, the wires were hot with messages from Washington to Pope and Army of the Potomac commander George McClellan, who was now headquartered near Alexandria, Virginia, after finally getting back from the peninsula in front of Richmond. Portions of his troops were already on the move to reinforce Pope.

Lincoln, seeking information and counsel, asked McClellan what he had heard. In one of the more controversial wires of the war, McClellan responded with his own advice, in part stating: "I am clear that one of two courses should be adopted: First, to concentrate all of our available forces to open communications with Pope: Second, to leave Pope to get out of his scrape, and at once use all our means to make the capital perfectly safe."[26] It would be interpreted by some in the days to follow that his words were almost treasonous by not fully recommending to support Pope, and did not sit well with Lincoln at all.

At 5:00 P.M. on the 29th, the last and best opportunity for Federal success occurred. The best successes of the day had been against the Confederate left, near Sudley Ford, so once again Pope would probe that area. Major General Philip Kearny, a tough forty-seven-year-old, one-armed veteran of the Mexican War, was ordered to lead his division against Jackson's left. He was able to significantly breach the Confederate line for the fourth time of the day, driving Confederate General A. P. Hill's men back beyond the Groveton-Sudley road (*modern Route 622*) before the Confederates held near the foot of Stoney Ridge. Yet again, Pope failed to send in reinforcements, thus near victory turned into retreat for the Federals. The 29th ended with some of the greatest carnage ever witnessed by American armies up to that point, yet both sides were essentially in the same position as when the day started. Pope was hopeful that his breakthroughs of the Confederate line, albeit brief ones, offered significant encouragement for the following day. His emphasis that night would again be attacking Jackson and his men in the center on the 30th.

Completely unbeknownst to Pope, however, Lee and General James Longstreet's corps had now arrived on the scene. Pope was unaware that Longstreet's corps had come all the way through Thoroughfare Gap and was now being placed by Lee on Pope's exposed left flank. Word began to filter to him in the early afternoon of August 30 of a large rebel buildup on his left, but he refused to believe it, to the point that Union General Fitz-John Porter's brigade was taken from the Union left flank to assist with the planned attack against the center.[27]

At mid-afternoon on August 30, 25,000 rebel troops came crashing out of the woods and into the Union left along Chinn Ridge. Hearing the high-pitched rebel yell all around them, Union troops began to flee in panic. One Yank recalled, "The companies barely had time to discharge their pieces once before the rebels were almost on top of them."[28] The Federals retreated back to Henry House Hill, primary sight of the first Bull Bun battle, and made a final, successful defensive stand before night relieved them of the Southern juggernaut. By 9:00 P.M. that evening, Federal forces were streaming across the stone bridge over Bull Run to safety.

March of Longstreet's corps through Thoroughfare Gap

The retreat over the stone bridge, Saturday evening, August 30

Battles and Leaders

Decades later, Private Henry Gerrish of the 7th New York would write to his grandson and say in a few words what had transpired over the previous two and one-half days: "It appeared that this battle had no other strategic meaning other than to give Pope and McDowell a very good thrashing, in which Jackson succeeded finely."[29]

Thoroughly whipped and beaten, but with his army still intact, John Pope ordered his men to march toward the secure Federal defenses up on Centreville ridge. Union morale had never been lower, and gloom amongst the bluecoats was rampant. Many believed they had fought hard and well against the Confederates, but once again their officers had been out-generaled. The entire fiasco cost the Union many lives of promising young lieutenants and captains. A New Hampshire private later wrote to his wife angrily counting off the number of officers in his regiment that had fallen: "Out of twenty commissioned officers that went into the fight only eight came out. Sharp shooters in the trees was death on officers."[30]

John Pope and his top lieutenant, Irvin McDowell, were disparaged openly. One of McDowell's New Yorkers wrote: "Such a march I never witnessed before and never want to again. Oh! How this defeat discouraged and discontented our men. They all said they would never fight again under McDowell, brave as they were they all said they could not fight with enthusiasm under McDowell."[31]

In the meantime, Pope was hot on the wire to Washington that all necessary defenses be taken to protect the capital. Pope was also making sure that his defensive breastworks were in a state of high readiness, prompting New York Private Robert Sneden to note: "Lanterns were seen moving all night on the old Rebel forts at Centreville, while the sound of hundreds of axes were heard on all sides."[32] Massachusetts Private Wilbur Fisk probably echoed the sentiments of the army when he wrote: "About midnight, we were back again to Centreville, and when the order came to rest, you may be sure we were in a condition to obey it with a hearty good will. It was beginning to rain, and there was a chilly east wind, and we were without any woolen blankets, having come in light marching order, but we made the best we could of our situation. If I felt any disposition to grumble at that time, I was sincerely ashamed of it the next morning, when I heard the boys engaged in the fight speak of their comrades whom they had been obliged to leave on the field, wounded and dying, without care or help from any source."[33]

Like a number of battles between Federals and Confederates, the battle of September 1, 1862, at Ox Hill has been known by two different names. Federal forces had the tradition of naming engagements after the nearest topographical feature, such as a river. In contrast, the Confederates usually named battles after the nearest town or village. What became known as the battles of Bull Run, Antietam Creek, and Stones River in the North, became known to Southerners respectively as Manassas, Sharpsburg, and Murfreesboro. Chantilly is unique in that this time the roles were reversed, with Union soldiers referring to it in the future as the battle of Chantilly while Confederates referred to it as the battle of Ox Hill. Ox Hill referred to the small rise in the land from where the Confederates dispersed and fought. A reason for this strange reversal can be postulated from the 1862 topographical map from which Union forces planned and operated. The neighboring estate and post office of Chantilly was prominently featured, yet the ridge of Ox Hill appears nowhere on the map. Union cartographers and engineers were not even aware of its existence! Yet Jedediah Hotchkiss, mapmaker to Stonewall Jackson, had the ridge noted prominently on his map of the area.[34] For the purpose of this work, the two names will be used interchangeably, with no preference being given to one name or the other.

"I suppose I've captured the dinner also!" **2**

Opening Movements—August 31, 1862

Lee Decides

Lee and his army were certainly flushed with the taste of victory. His army had delivered to the Federals their worst whipping of the war to date, but he was far from satisfied. He had Pope's army on the ropes; his goal was now to militarily destroy "those people,"[1] not merely defeat them. His scouts and cavalry were all reporting on the incessantly overcast and rainy morning of August 31 that Union troops were streaming up Centreville Ridge and into their fortifications. This told Lee that no further offensive action was to be immediately forthcoming from his foe. He realized that Pope was now on the defensive, but how to get at him? Lee knew that the Centreville fortifications were formidable, as much of them had been built by the Confederates the previous winter. Perhaps thinking back to the Confederate disaster earlier that spring at Malvern Hill, Lee realized that any head-on assault against Yankee cannon would be foolhardy. Colonel Asbury Coward of the 5th South Carolina realized this as well, writing: "In the grayish light we got a view of Centreville Heights, bristling with cannon of the heaviest caliber. Outside the lines were batteries massed so that the whole sloping plain of three points of a circle could be swept."[2]

To the south lay Bull Run, which was swollen from heavy rains, thereby making crossing difficult, plus the roads in that direction were poor. Lee also learned that Union General Nathaniel Banks' II Corps, Army of Virginia, was coming their way from Manassas to reinforce, and rumored to be guarding Pope's communication lines near Fairfax. A flanking movement northward to once again get in Pope's rear

17

seemed to be the logical choice. The roads were better in that direction and there would be fewer streams to cross. If Pope realized the Confederates were getting behind him, it would force him to leave his Centreville stronghold. The potential risks to Lee and his army were nominal. If Pope responded with any degree of aggression to block the flanking maneuver, or if superior numbers of Union troops were to be forthcoming from either Washington or Alexandria, Lee knew he could always fall back into Loudoun County and consider advancing northward into Maryland.

With much to gain and little to lose, Lee made his decision. On the morning of August 31 he ordered Stonewall Jackson, master of the flank attack, to take his entire command and first head north, and then southeast to flank the Union army's right wing, thereby placing himself between Washington and the Federals. Longstreet, whose corps was farthest from the departure point, was to follow. When General Daniel H. Hill's division arrived from the south the Confederates could deliver the final crushing blow to Pope. Upon hearing of Lee's orders, Jackson reportedly shouted "Good!" and rode away to prepare.[3] A day of desperately needed rest and recuperation would not be forthcoming for the exhausted men of Jackson's wing. The fatigue and exhaustion caused by forced marches and desperate battles in the past week would become plainly evident over the next twenty-four hours.

Robert E. Lee, on the other hand, would be riding nowhere on a horse for several weeks. With it still raining, the general was attired in a rubber poncho and overalls, and was dismounted in woods discussing strategy with several of his officers. Believing Yankee cavalry to be approaching, he quickly stepped forward to grab his horse's rein and inadvertently tripped on his bulky clothing and fell forward harshly onto his outstretched hands. The result was a broken bone in one hand and a severe sprain in the other. For several weeks he would be forced to wear splints on each wrist and was required to ride in an ambulance. That resulted in widespread rumor in Northern papers of his condition. Some erroneously reported that he had been wounded in battle while others stated that he had been wounded in the hand by the accidental discharge of his own pistol.[4] It can only be speculated what course history might have taken had he been able to ride along with Jackson.

Confederate General James Longstreet's wing was ordered to stay behind at the Manassas battlefield to serve as a diversion to keep Pope's forces pinned down, in order to allow Jackson ample time to get behind Pope. Longstreet would then rapidly follow behind Jackson the next day. To accomplish this distraction, Longstreet had the brigade of Brigadier General Roger Pryor cross Bull Run around noon where they demonstrated against Union positions while occupying the high ground between that stream and Cub Run.[5] A few Yankee shells from General Jesse Reno's batteries helped to scatter the Confederate pickets, and then rebel artillery would respond with equal enthusiasm. For the most part, the Northerners on Centreville ridge were out of sight of the Confederate gunners. Nevertheless Private Nicholas Rice of the 50th Pennsylvania recalled that "many of their shells burst over and around us, and some would strike the ground well in front, lose part of their momentum, and come bouncing and skipping toward us—rather harmless looking things—but their was force enough left to knock a leg off, or cut a man in twain."[6] Despite the occasional cannonade and the light skirmishing in the Cub Run valley, the main intent of Lee's strategy was playing out; Pope was making sure a very sizable force remained at Centreville to keep an eye on Longstreet's wing.[7]

Other units under Longstreet served to help with the wounded, collect arms and ammunition, and begin the grim work of burying the fallen. One rebel took careful note of the process: "A large pit is dug, usually about thirty feet long and seven feet wide, but miserably

View of the fortifications on the Centreville heights, taken only six months prior to the battle of Ox Hill. Note the desolation.

Library of Congress

shallow, its depth seldom exceeding two or three feet. A rail is then provided and to it, at an interval of about five feet, are attached two nooses. The head and feet of the dead soldier (who has become stiff by this time) are inserted in these loops, and the extremities of the rail, projecting beyond the loops, being placed upon the shoulders of two men of the burying detail, the corpse is borne and deposited upon the banks of the pit. When a sufficient number of bodies has thus been collected, they are placed in the pit crosswise and parallel with each other, and the earth heaped over them. The spectacle of a hundred detachments doing this work at the same time will always make a forcible impression on the novice's mind."[8]

Many rebels viewed the Yankee dead as a better source than their own quartermasters for outfitting themselves. One Virginian proudly boasted, "I got us about twenty Enfield rifle muskets for my company and several good oil cloths and blankets."[9] As usual, the ragged rebels mused that since the Union dead no longer had a need for their clothing, shoes, or the other accoutrements of war, such as tents, a quick sweep of the field of all usable personal items was justified before marching on. Even Confederate surgeons joined the fray, seeking out always needed medical supplies. Those simple farmers from the South who walked or rode over the Manassas battlefield following Second Bull Run saw a nightmarish vision of carnage and destruction they remembered for the rest of their days. "It was the most horrible sight I ever beheld in all the days of my life," wrote a Virginia cavalryman to his sibling. "The dead Yankees were lying thick as rocks & they had been lying there for 3 days, they had turned as black as Negroes." A Georgian who marched over the Manassas battlefield three days later remarked: "There was not a Yankee left with a pair of shoes on and a few had every rag of clothes taken off."[10]

One rebel soldier on burial detail observed that morning how he noticed that the Confederate dead were "in much better condition" than their Union counterparts. He calculated that as the Union troops had been much better fed, therefore fatter, they decomposed much more quickly than their leaner rebel counterparts. "The difference was so marked that in places the lines of battle could be distinguished by the color of the dead."[11] It was an accurate analysis, for both quantity and quality of food was higher in the Union army than in the Confederate. A captured, full Yankee haversack was a prized possession, but on this day many rebels were merrily eating straight from the abandoned Yankee stockpots. The Union skedaddle had been so quick that cautious rebel pickets entering Federal camps found that they appeared to be still in use. "In many cases we came to their camps where they have even left their meat boiling on the fire—and there stand the kettles with boiled beef and bacon still in them, sometimes scarcely cold."[12] The dead and missing would have no need for those meals. And the dead were plainly everywhere. Artillerist Edward Moore calculated that he could have walked a quarter of a mile in a straight line in front of the railroad cut on the dead Federals without ever touching the ground. "The area presented the appearance of an immense flower garden, the prevailing blue thickly dotted with red, the color of the Federal Zouave uniform." He spoke for the Army of Northern Virginia when he realized that such scenes "disabused us of the idea that the Northerners would not fight."[13]

As was the case at Cedar Mountain, a truce requested by Pope had been granted by the Confederates, this time by Lee, so that Pope's soldiers could bury dead and care for the wounded. A ceasefire of only a few hours was allowed, so the long train of Federal ambulances had to quickly snake their way over the Manassas

Between the lines during a truce

Battles and Leaders

Plains, picking up all the fallen that they could. When they had gone, the Confederates could still see scores of Federal dead. "We gathered up the dead by wagon loads and threw them into a cut in the railroad—hundreds together."[14]

Around midday on Sunday, August 31, Jackson's weary and hungry "foot cavalry" splashed across Sudley Ford and began their trek northward up the Gum Springs Road *(modern Route 659),* then a single-track dirt country road, which would lead them to the Little River Turnpike *(modern Route 50).* It was still overcast and raining steadily, so the march was slowed considerably more by the muddy road, as well as by soldier fatigue.

Longstreet later wrote of the road conditions during his corps' march that "If Jackson had been followed by an enemy whose march he wished to baffle, his gun-carriages could not have made deeper cuts through the mud and quicksand."[15] Approximately 15,000 men were now on the move, with A. P. Hill's light division in the lead. The usually fast-moving Jackson had chided Hill in the past for advancing too slowly, but on this occasion Hill's vanguard got so far in front that Jackson would later admonish Hill for moving too swiftly, stating that Hill "permitted the head of his columns again to march too rapidly and allowed a large number of men to straggle from the ranks."[16] The Jackson-Hill feud showed no signs of abating. As was usually the case in the war, the soldiers had no idea of their ultimate destination. "There is much speculation, but no knowledge of our destination," wrote one of the Confederates.[17]

Cavalry Skirmishes

As the eyes and ears of the army, Confederate General James E. B. Stuart's cavalry was the first to head out on the morning of August 31 to ascertain enemy positions. So expeditious had been the Yankee retreat the previous evening that the cavalry brigades of Generals Beverly Robertson and Fitzhugh Lee seemed to meet with nothing except a few stragglers and twenty to thirty ambulances until they were within range of the Federal guns near Centreville.[18] Though the rebel cavalrymen could easily see the white tents of the Federal soldiers perched atop the distant ridgeline, they were not expecting to find the small contingent of Union rearguard cavalry and artillery posted in their path on the other side of Cub Run bridge.

General Ambrose Powell Hill

Miller, *Photographic History of the Civil War*

Mounted Federal skirmishers quickly began to ford the stream as the Confederate sharpshooters took their positions. The clattering of carbine fire commenced as Stuart's horse artillery pounded up into position. Just as Stuart formed his men into line for a charge, the Union skirmish line broke and began retiring back across Cub Run. Explosions rocked the ground near the Confederate line as the Union artillery on the Centreville heights began to open up. Captain John Pelham's rebel artillery quickly responded, which soon quieted the Union guns. In the mud and drizzle, Stuart's relatively unabated patrol continued.[19]

This virtual free ride of Stuart's troopers was due in large mea-sure to a total breakdown of the Union cavalry due to fatigue. Pope

urgently requested two thousand fresh mounts from Halleck at midday of the 31st, and later in the early hours of September 1 Pope
would again wire Halleck: "We have no cavalry—not a horse that
can possibly perform service" and three hours later at 8:45 A.M.: "Our
cavalry is completely broken down, so that there are not five horses
to a company that can raise a trot. The consequence is that I am
forced to keep considerable infantry along the roads in my rear to
make them secure, and even then it is difficult to keep the enemy's
cavalry off the roads."[20]

After fully scouting the area, the rebel cavalry was to concentrate near the once elegant plantation known as "Chantilly," which
lay along the Little River Turnpike north of Centreville. The plantation originally had been owned by Richard Henry Lee, a hero of the
American Revolution who died there in 1794. Now it was owned by
Charles Calvert Stuart, a member of the pre-war Virginia legislature
and who had been labeled by Federal authorities as "a shrewd, cool,
dangerous Secesh who was not to be trusted."[21] With the initial se-
cession of Virginia, the home had been refuge to several friends of
the family abandoning Union-controlled Alexandria. Among them,
Judith McGuire had noted in her journal the exquisiteness of the
place, but also a sense of dread that inevitably proved correct: "Nature and art have combined to make this one of the most beautiful
spots I ever saw, yet we look upon it sadly, fearing that the trail of the
serpent may pass over it all....The ladies of the family are here all
alone. The sons are where they should be, in the [Confederate]
camp."[22] As war had swept over the area over the past year, the
family had fled southward to safety, and therefore, the now vacant
home had been used by Union authorities as a field hospital and
headquarters. By the time of the Confederate cavalry's arrival that
morning, it had long since become a ghost of its former self. One
Southern infantryman who arrived too late for the coming battle later
mourned as he marched by the house: "We beheld the evidence so
plain before our eyes of the sacked and ruined Chantilly; that sweet,
lovely place which, for nearly a century, had been famous for all that
makes a home prized and loved, and an estate cared for and valued. The fences were all leveled, the outbuildings were demolished,
the splendid park cut down—every shade tree was felled by the axe,
even the fruit trees were hacked down out of mere wantonness. As
for the house, it was hardly habitable, the furniture was smashed to

The Ayre stone house

This last surviving building of Civil War-era Chantilly was possibly the home of the plantation overseer.

Collection of the author

kindling wood, the windows dashed to pieces with the butt end of the muskets, the plastering from the walls knocked off, and the rooms so defaced and defiled that it discounted a hog pen in filth."[23] Due to its predominance, the name "Chantilly" had spread to the surrounding countryside as well, even becoming the official name of a nearby post office and tavern that served travelers on the Little River Turnpike.

Contact between the scouts and pickets of both sides commenced and grew throughout the 31st just north of Centreville. Emma Machen, whose prominent family owned a large farm in the vicinity that they called "Walney," wrote of the 31st to her brother: "we have been almost in the midst of battles. Indeed a cavalry charge was made in our corn field, and troops were drawn up in line of battle in our northwest field. The uncertainty whether cannon balls and shells might not be falling about us at any moment added not a little to our unpleasant situation, especially after the theft of our horses and oxen left us entirely without the means of moving if the danger to life had seemed so imminent." Emma would later lightheartedly refer to the destruction of their farm as "the Battle of Walney."[24]

The 2nd U.S. Cavalry, which had been the old unit of Fitzhugh Lee, was being led by Captain Thomas Hight that afternoon and was patrolling the area north of Centreville, having received orders to reconnoiter the far right of the Union position as far as the "nearly destroyed village of Germantown,"[25] and then return to Centreville. Their initial scouting route took them north up Walney Road, which was the primary north-south road from Centreville at the time. Hight's maps or knowledge of the area apparently was of marginal quality, as he reported that ultimately he realized that Germantown was two or three miles to his rear, and headed east down the Little River Turnpike in that direction. After stopping to rest, his unit was unexpectedly charged from the rear by the Confederate cavalry forces of Fitz Lee, approximately one-quarter mile east of Stringfellow Road. Caught completely unaware, Hight later lamented that "there was nothing left for me but surrender or massacre." Though Hight's report indicated that the stop was for the rest and feeding of his horses, Fitz Lee later asserted that it was the prospect of a hot meal for the officers at a local farmhouse that prompted the halt. Regarding that costly meal the general good-naturedly remarked to his prisoners: "Well, as I've captured the party ordering it, I suppose I've captured the dinner also! I cordially invite you gentlemen to partake of it as my guests!"[26] Of this affair, a Confederate participant recalled, "There was little fighting to be done. We rushed so suddenly and unexpectedly upon the Yankee reserves that they had not even time to mount, and two full companies with their officers fell into our hands. We captured also their horses, from among which I lost no time in exchanging a noble bay for my own worn out animal."[27]

Indicative of Robert E. Lee's disdain for Pope was his order that none of Pope's officers were to be paroled, if captured. As Fitz Lee was unaware whether these men were from McClellan's Army of the Potomac or Pope's Army of Virginia, he simply detained them all until after the battle, at which time they were permitted to withdraw to the lines at Washington.[28] The capture of Hight and his troopers was reported by the few Federals who managed to escape. Their report back to Union headquarters contributed to the growing concern about Confederate activity north of the Union position. Shortly after this capture, Jeb Stuart along with Robertson's brigade arrived to hook up with Fitz Lee's cavalry brigade near the old Chantilly mansion.

Hight's and the 2nd U.S.'s capture were only the first of two troublesome episodes for the Yankee cavalry that day. A company of the 10th New York Cavalry, assigned to the defenses of Washington, had been on patrol that afternoon scouting as far north as Dranesville and then heading south through Herndon Station and Frying Pan. At approximately 8:00 P.M., when they were but several miles north of Centreville, they were ordered to stop ostensibly by pickets of the 1st Pennsylvania Cavalry, but which turned out to be elements of Robertson's 12th Virginia Cavalry. After being lured forward, the Federal troopers were surrounded by a larger force of Confederates and without a gun being fired, the entire company of approximately thirty men was captured save one, who, after purportedly killing his two captors with a concealed knife, managed to weave his way back to Fairfax on horse and report the episode.[29]

Near sunset Confederate scouts had reported back to Stuart that Federal supply trains were making their way east toward Germantown, rumbling down the Warrenton Turnpike *(modern route 29)*. The wagons were also accompanied by the 1st and 3rd New Jersey Infantry[30] which made a direct attack imprudent; but Stuart obviously could not stand the thought of allowing them to pass unmolested. The 9th Virginia Cavalry was ordered to form in line of battle in a hidden ravine near the turnpike in case a full engagement broke out. Stuart then ordered two guns from 1st Company of the Washington Artillery brought up. Shortly thereafter, "the artillery was placed in position just after dark, and opened upon the road."[31] The gunners no doubt knew their work well, for in the words of Stuart's staff officer, Major Heros von Borcke: "the artillery soon began to perform great execution on the long line of wagons, whose white tops we could see, through the dusk of evening, winding slowly along the road like a gigantic snake. The confusion in a few minutes became bewildering, as the balls from our guns went crashing through the heavily laden vans, and the loud cries of the drivers vainly endeavoring to get out of range commingled in a tumultuous din with the disorderly commands of the officers of the supporting force."[32] Stuart was no doubt pleased with himself, but it can be surmised that Lee would not have been, for prior to the shelling, his flanking plan had a high probability of success, but after, it was diminished as further evidence was given to Union leaders of the rebel buildup on their right. Lee would certainly have echoed the sentiments of Union General George Meade, who months later would comment to

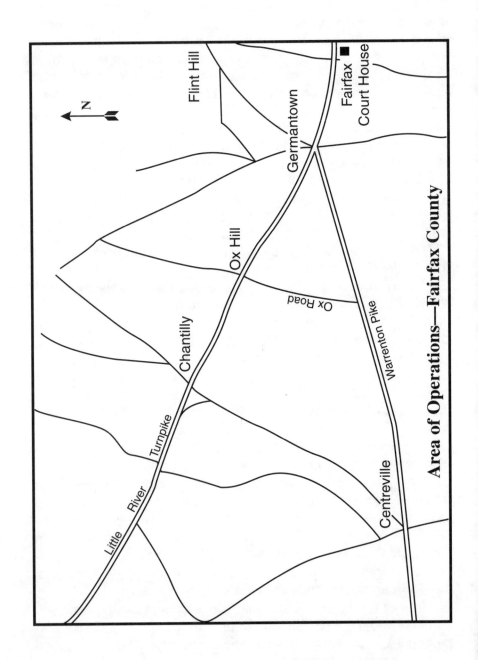

Area of Operations—Fairfax County

General "Jeb" Stuart, Confederate cavalry

His reckless shelling of a Union wagon train may have cost Jackson's Confederate infantry the crucial element of surprise.

a subordinate on a similar opportunity, but different engagement, "Yes! [and] what good would you do? [but] scare a few old...mules?"[33]

John Moore, in his 1964 article on the battle of Chantilly, aptly concluded: "Stuart's mission was to uncover information while denying it to the Federal cavalry and remaining as inconspicuous as possible. It is difficult to see how he could have done less damage and created more alarm while collecting a minimum of information.... Information was available at every farmhouse; many of his men were natives. Stuart himself had picketed the area the previous summer, fall, and winter."[34] It would not be the last time in his career that the twenty-nine-year-old cavalier would undertake such costly and controversial actions.

Following the shelling of the Yankee wagon train, Stuart and his troopers retired for the night near the Chantilly village, arriving there around 10 P.M. Obviously pleased with himself and filled with a desire for revelry, the happy-go-lucky Stuart and his staff paid a visit to the home of some old family friends who lived nearby and made merry that night.[35]

Pope Contemplates

After getting his troops behind the old rebel fortifications along Centreville ridge,[36] Pope's primary goal that morning became one of defense, at least until he could reorganize his army and await the arrival of more soldiers from the Army of the Potomac who were now en route from Alexandria and the peninsula. General William B. Franklin's VI Corps from the Army of the Potomac had just arrived, much to the relief of Pope. According to Pope, his defensive positions were as follows: "Porter (9000 strong) to occupy the entrenchments on the north or right of Centreville; Franklin on his left, in the entrenchments. In rear of Centreville, between Franklin and Porter, as a support, was posted the corps of Heintzelman. Sigel occupied the entrenchments on the left and south side of the town, with Reno on his left and rear. Banks was ordered to take post, as soon as he arrived, on the north side of Bull Run, and to cover the bridge on the road from Centreville to Manassas Junction. Sumner, as soon as he arrived from Washington, was ordered to take post between Centreville and Chantilly, and to occupy Chantilly in force. McDowell was posted about two miles in the rear of Centerville, on the road to Fairfax Court-House." At most, it would be a day of resting and waiting as far as John Pope was concerned.[37]

Not all were enthused by Pope's apparent plan to sit still at Centreville. Army of the Potomac General Fitz-John Porter wired to his friend and confidant General George McClellan in Alexandria: "I expect to hear hourly of our rear being cut and our supplies and trains at Fairfax Station (scarcely guarded) being destroyed, as we are required to stay here and fight."[38]

Pope's moods seemed to swing throughout the day. His defeatism on the 31st was growing by the hour, and his dispatches of the day to Union General in Chief Henry Halleck back in Washington were revealing. By mid-morning he was inquiring of Halleck the status of Washington's defenses should his army in the field be destroyed. Pope informed Halleck that his army "would fight to the last," and claimed that Confederate General "Ewell is killed, Jackson is badly wounded, and other generals of less note wounded."[39] Whether or not Pope ever contemplated renewing the offensive at this time against Lee is not clear. He certainly had the fresh troops to work with as almost 25,000 men from the Army of the Potomac were arriving as early as the evening before. Halleck had even sent word to Pope wondering if the attack could not be renewed.[40] It is not known if Pope personally visited the makeshift hospitals within Centreville on that depressing day of August 31, but if he did, it could only have added further to his lack of offensive resolve. A Union cavalryman who had seen the horror the previous day later recalled: "There were no bandages, no stores, no nurses, no provision for any of the contingencies of surgical practice.... The very wells, from which alone could be drawn water to assuage the agonizing thirst of the wounded, had been broken and rendered useless by wanton soldiery; and there, on the rough floor, with no beds, no straw, no covering, the poor sufferers had to endure the fever-increasing thirst in aggravation of their paroxysms of pain. Officers and men together were dropped down wherever there was room for them to lie, in order that the overdriven ambulances might return to the field for more. No one knew where to apply for assistance; no one knew how to obtain food; no one knew where to look for orders."[41] Whatever thoughts passed through Pope's mind at midday, it became increasingly evident that the Union offensive would not, could not, be renewed. A visitor to Pope's farmhouse headquarters in the afternoon of August 31 recalled a scene of despair: "I shall never forget the striking appearance of the commander-in-chief. He sat with his chair tipped back against the wall, his hands clasped behind his head, which bent forward, his chin touching his breast,—seeming to pay no attention to the generals as they arrived, but to be wholly wrapped in his own gloomy reflections."[42]

By nightfall on the 31st Pope's confusion must have been deep and depressing. It could not have been helped upon receiving a letter from General Joseph Hooker stating that "It is my duty to report for the information of the major-general commanding the corps that my division is in no condition to meet the enemy. This was communicated to me yesterday by my brigade commanders, and on inquiry I find their morale to be such as to warrant me in entertaining the most serious apprehension of their conduct in their present state."[43]

Pope's pessimism had even spread to the staff officers, one man lamenting in his diary, "If we ever reach Washington in safety, it will be more than I expect."[44]

The lot of the average Yankee private at Centreville that miserable day was pitiable. His self-appointed, primary mission was to find something to eat and stay as dry as possible. Many of the men had not slept for two nights, had endured a forced march the night before from the Bull Run battlefield, and were overcome with fatigue and hunger. Scores were shivering in their wet uniforms from having to ford Bull Run, which was neck-deep during the retreat. The cold rain that continued to fall on the dreary, overcast day added the final punctuation to their sense of misery and defeat. The 51st Pennsylvania helped to alleviate their despair by absconding with dry clothing that had belonged to a German regiment. A Pennsylvanian later remarked that "their woeful looking countenances bespoke the sad disappointment they felt at their loss, and their 'Cod fer tams' were frequent and loud." The Pennsylvanian justified the pilfering by noting that while the Germans had their dry tents to return to, the Pennsylvania men were still forced to lie in the bitter rain without food. A fellow comrade noted that lack of food was possibly a moot point, for not a stick or chip of wood could be found with which to build a fire.[45]

The activity on the Union right was now too great for even Pope to ignore. News of Jackson's men coming down the Little River Turnpike was reaching him by now. The pike had to be blocked or else, Pope knew by now, the Confederate plan to flank his right would work. He was painfully familiar with Lee's tendencies and was not going to be caught off guard again, and advised Halleck of his resolve.[46] Yet, in total, his actions were far from decisive. Instead of ordering substantial infantry to move north and block the pike, only a reconnaissance was ordered. At 3:00 A.M., September 1, Pope fired off the following order to Major General Edwin Sumner: "The reconnoitering party of cavalry which you sent out yesterday morning, under Captain Hight, has, as I am informed, been captured by the enemy's cavalry. It is essential that your right be carefully watched. I desire you at daylight to push a reconnaissance of not less than one brigade, supported, if necessary, by a second, toward the north of your position, to the Little River Turnpike and beyond. The direction of your reconnaissance should be as nearly due north as practicable, and should be pushed not less than five miles. It is of great importance that this reconnaissance should be made at an early hour in the morning."[47]

The carrying out of this order was handed to General Oliver Otis Howard and the "Philadelphia Brigade," which consisted of the 69th, 71st, 72nd, and 106th Pennsylvania Regiments. They set out on the planned reconnaissance and encountered little opposition, with Howard noting, "We marched rapidly till we aroused Lee's pickets. They gave way; then we came in sight of his skirmishers, who opened fire upon us at once. When we had pressed them more closely, we succeeded in drawing the fire of their noisy batteries." Believing their mission to be accomplished, Howard and his brigade opted to return to their tents after a march of only several miles.[48] About three hours later, at 5:45 A.M., he further advised Sumner that "the reconnaissance is only designed to ascertain whether there is any considerable movement of the enemy's infantry toward our right and rear...I do not care that the brigade shall be pushed further than the Little River turnpike, whilst skirmishers are thrown still farther, in order fully to ascertain whether the enemy is making any movement toward Germantown and Fairfax Court House. I do not wish any engagement brought on at present on that ground, but when the information required shall have been obtained by the brigade withdraw it."[49]

A Frustrated Jackson

Jackson and his men finally reached the turnpike after dark, after covering only ten miles in eight hours, which were poor results for the vaunted foot cavalry. They turned right and were now marching in

Supper after a hard march

Scribners Monthly/ Battles and Leaders

a southeasterly direction. Exhausted men dropped where they stood when the corps finally halted for the night around 10 P.M. The lead regiments bivouacked in fields one mile from the turn, near the small church and village of Pleasant Valley.[50] Other units lagged as far back as Gum Springs, including the ration trains, so the vanguard of Jackson's men went to sleep in the rain and mud that night on empty stomachs. The lucky few who found some roasting ears of corn ate them happily.[51] There was a great degree of straggling, surely due to sheer exhaustion from the concluded three-day battle at Manassas along with the drizzling rain, so for the time being Jackson was forced to abandon the initiative.

Meanwhile, Longstreet's men finally ended up leaving the Manassas battlefield late in the afternoon with most of them camping for the night at Sudley's Ford, where Jackson had begun earlier that morning.[52] Longstreet's men were at least able to have some rations that night. Most men received a meager meal of two hard-tack crackers and a quarter-pound of bacon.[53]

Hunger and lack of sleep can make even the most honorable men resort to desperate measures. The Confederate march from

Sudley Springs up the Gum Springs Road and then east/southeast down the Little River Turnpike was no exception. Many of these men had not eaten nor slept properly in days, and the hunger and fatigue were starting to take their toll. It would become even more apparent in the next twenty-four hours. The Virginia landscape had been ravaged by more than a year of heavy fighting and its barren fields and stark appearance were evident everywhere. One soldier described it as "bleak fields and forests with scarce a roof visible in the entire landscape...a solemn or mysterious air reigned over this wide, desolate flat plain."[54]

That night, in the privacy of his tent, Jackson wrote to his wife, Anna: "We were engaged with the enemy at and near Manassas Junction Tuesday and Wednesday, and again near the battlefield of Manassas on Thursday, Friday and Saturday; in all of which God gave us the victory. May He ever be with us, and we ever be His devoted people, is my earnest prayer. It greatly encourages me to feel that so many of God's people are praying for that part of our force under my command."[55]

"I think we will have a fight before night"   3

Early Morning to Mid-Afternoon—September 1, 1862

Jackson and the "Foot Cavalry" Move Out

The vanguard of Jackson's men began leisurely moving out from Pleasant Valley around 7:00 A.M. on the morning of September 1, with the old "Stonewall" division in the lead, now commanded by General William E. Starke. Starke had been forced to take over for General William B. Taliaferro, who had been severely wounded early on in the fighting at Second Manassas. It was followed closely by General Alexander R. Lawton's division. Recently promoted like Starke, Lawton had just replaced Richard Ewell as head of the division due to Ewell's serious leg wound three days prior at Bull Run. General A. P. Hill still had command of his light division and was bringing up the rear of the column.[1] Even though the rebel goal of sneaking in behind Pope's rear called for swiftness and daring, a lack of urgency seemed to be the order of the new dawn. Private William McClendon from the 15th Alabama of Trimble's brigade recollected of that morning, "The officers high in authority didn't seem to be in any great hurry, and we were given plenty of time to make coffee and eat breakfast."[2]

Two columns marched on either side of the wide road, with the artillery moving down the middle. This type of march was generally viewed by the soldiers as more pleasing than on the road, as it allowed them to venture over meadows and grass as opposed to a cloud of dust. It also allowed for quicker dispersion into fighting formations. Jackson's corps was now heading in an east-southeast direction down the Little River Turnpike. That road was everything

36

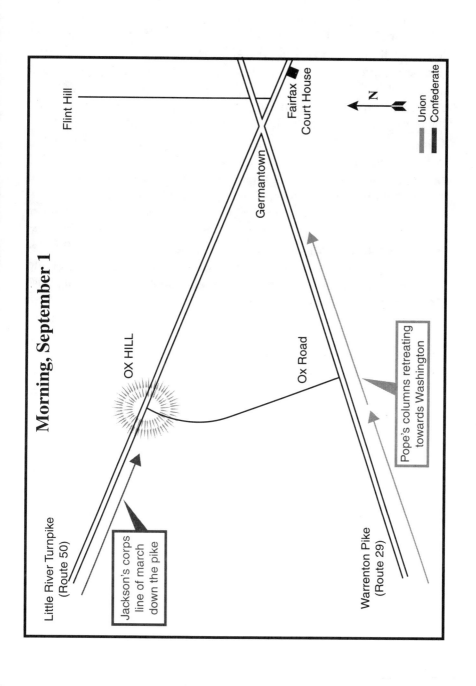

Morning, September 1

Flint Hill

Little River Turnpike
(Route 50)

OX HILL

Germantown

Fairfax
Court House

Jackson's corps
line of march
down the pike

Ox Road

Warrenton Pike
(Route 29)

Pope's columns retreating
towards Washington

N

Union
Confederate

their previous day's muddied cart path was not. Built in the early 1800s, the pike was a thirty-foot-wide, wood- and-gravel-covered toll road that embodied state-of-the-art road building of that era. Jackson's men and artillery certainly had ample room for their morning march.

Jackson's most pertinent concern at the moment was securing his right flank against a possible Union strike from the south at Centreville. To achieve that goal, General William Starke, whose division was in the fore, sent Campbell's brigade, now commanded by Colonel Bradley T. Johnson, to hold Stringfellow Road, which ran from Centreville to Chantilly. Half of the 21st Virginia under Captain William Witcher was sent out on Jackson's front and right, south of the turnpike, to act as skirmishers with their line set up about two and a half miles from Centreville. Their wait was not long, for elements of George Bayard's New Jersey cavalry had been suspecting just such an advance and were out early scouting the countryside. This run-and-shoot skirmishing west of Ox Hill would continue for the better part of the morning and early afternoon, but as Johnson's men were ordered only to observe the large Federal host in front of them, they were content to hold their thin line.[3]

Meanwhile, Longstreet's men were finally crossing Bull Run back at Sudley Ford in an attempt to hook up with Jackson, consequently the attempted flanking maneuver was now fully under way, albeit slowly. "Ol' Pete's" men seemed to have a better time with food than Jackson's. One soldier noted that "our breakfast that morning consisted of beef, sliced off by us as we hurriedly passed the smoking carcass, slaughtered by the enemy a short time previous."[4] Proper distribution of rations appears to have been problematic within A. P. Hill's division as some men in General Maxcy Gregg's South Carolina brigade were at the point of mutiny, swearing they would not continue to march without food. A wagon with some barrels of crackers was found and ordered back whereupon three crackers were issued to each man. Apparently this was sufficient to allay their hunger as their march continued.[5] Conversely, soldiers within Trimble's brigade seemed quite satisfied, one noting that "our supply that we had provided ourselves with over at Manassas had not been exhausted, and besides that, we had access to the well-filled haversacks of the dead boys in blue, so that there was nothing short in the ration department at that time."[6] This contentment was the unique exception, rather than the rule.

Jackson met Jeb Stuart that morning near the Chantilly mansion. Stuart had first reconnoitered to the northwest near Frying Pan Church and then moved south to rendezvous and inform Jackson of the previous day's activities and the situation as then known. Jackson could not have been pleased with Stuart's news. Though reporting the capture of two Federal cavalry units, the negative details included the ongoing buildup of Union troops near Germantown. In addition, Pope still had a sizeable force at Centreville that could threaten Jackson's right flank, the Warrenton Pike was jammed with

Sketch of General Thomas J. "Stonewall" Jackson

The Soldier in Our Civil War

men and teamsters, and Longstreet was apparently delayed as most of his men were still crossing Bull Run back at Sudley Ford.[7] Jackson was continuously compelled to move slowly as his weary, famished troops were still straggling and continuously looking for food. Jedediah Hotchkiss, mapmaker for Stonewall Jackson, noted in his journal on September 1 that "The soldiers were very bad, stealing everything eatable they could lay their hands on, after trying to buy it. They were nearly famished, our wagons being still behind. They were also very thirsty, water being very scarce. I had a hard time to keep them out of the house where I was at work."[8] The swift flanking move down the turnpike was not becoming one of the "foot cavalry's" finest moments. A soldier remarked in frustration that "Our march was slow, with frequent stops, sometimes lasting as long as an hour, as if to give time to our generals to locate the true positions of the enemy."[9] Finally, it was becoming clear as a result of repeated skirmishes with dismounted Federal cavalry and infantry pickets on Jackson's front and right that their whereabouts, and therefore Confederate intentions, were becoming known to the Union command.[10]

As the heavy, low-lying clouds again darkened ominously, Jackson's column halted once more and rested around midday near a small crest known to locals as Ox Hill.[11] The vaunted foot cavalry, certainly footsore, exhausted, and hungry from the maelstrom at Second Manassas, had only eked out another seven miles in about four hours. Here they stopped for several hours, no doubt due to the increased pressure being applied by Federal skirmishers and to await the arrival of Longstreet, lest a serious engagement break out. By early afternoon the rest of the corps had come up and now rested on the turnpike with Starke's leading brigade positioned just east of Ox Hill.

It was becoming increasingly apparent that the flanking maneuver was being exposed, and that either reinforcements or a change of plan would be in order. Having decided to wait for Longstreet, at that point Jackson gave Pope his first real break of the day. In an incident reminiscent of the Seven Days, the thirty-eight-year-old general proceeded to sit down under a tree, pulled his tattered VMI kepi down over his eyes, and took a much-needed nap.[12] This was not the action of a general who intended to add to his reputation as a master of the lightning flank attack, but rather that of a commander who was as physically drained as his men and intended to wait.

The men as well had a chance for some relaxing and good-natured humor. Ex-Virginia governor "Extra Billy" Smith, the colonel of the 49th Virginia, had a well-known disdain for military uniform and professional West Pointers. His favorite attire included a tall stove-pipe beaver hat atop what passed for his uniform. This morning Smith appeared in fine form as he donned his top hat and smilingly cavorted among the troops with his trademark blue umbrella fully extended, perhaps sensing the changing weather. His men could not contain themselves, shouting out, "Come out of that umbrel', I see your legs! Come out of that hat!, I want to boil the beans in it!"[13]

Federal Reinforcing at Germantown

Whatever little information General Edwin Sumner had obtained from his reconnaissance was done without any real contact with the Confederates. Jeb Stuart reported that he encountered no Union force other than a small cavalry patrol nearer than Centreville and that his men held Ox Hill up until Jackson's arrival.[14] Nevertheless, the continuous contact between Union cavalry and Jackson's skirmishers gave Pope the first hard evidence of Confederate intentions. As the new day dawned with cloudy and cool conditions, Pope was now assertively taking actions to ensure that his flank would not be turned. Discussions of the evening before between Pope and his generals had reached the conclusion that retreat was necessary, so immediately after breakfast, orders were given for the army to retire as fast as possible back to Alexandria.[15] Due to the news of Stuart's shelling of his wagon trains near Germantown, Pope had sent an entire brigade under Colonel Edward Hinks, which consisted of the 7th Michigan, 19th and 20th Massachusetts, and 42nd New York, along with two batteries, to reinforce the Union line at Germantown, which already had the New Jersey brigade under the command of Colonel Alfred Torbert from Franklin's division. On his march to join Pope at Centreville, Franklin had left the Jersey men at Fairfax at the behest of Army of the Potomac commander George McClellan, who deemed Fairfax to be a prime location for a blocking force. Hinks' brigade had arrived around 8:00 A.M. the morning of September 1, and two regiments immediately went out to picket.[16]

It is likely that Pope was well aware of his army's, not to mention his career's, predicament by the morning of September 1. His messages of the day were a preparation for the defense of his actions, and the ultimate pinning of blame elsewhere. In his wire at 8:50 A.M., after first briefly discussing the need for rest and horses, Pope, seemingly out of the blue, and to the probable dismay of Halleck, made known his emotions regarding subordinates from the Army of the Potomac, though he would not name them at this point: "I think it my duty to call your attention to the unsoldierly and dangerous conduct of many brigade and some division commanders of the forces sent here from the Peninsula. Every word and act and intention is discouraging, and calculated to break down the spirits of the men and produce disaster....You have hardly an idea of the demoralization among officers of high rank in the Potomac Army, arising in all instances from personal feeling in relation to changes of commander-in-chief and others. These men are mere tools or parasites, but their example is producing, and must necessarily produce, very disastrous results...." Pope concluded with his main point: "My advice to you—I give it with freedom, as I know you will not misunderstand it—is that, in view of any satisfactory results, you draw back this army to the intrenchments in front of Washington, and set to work in that secure place to reorganize and rearrange it. You may avoid great disaster by doing so."[17] Simply put, Pope was urging a full scale military retreat because in his mind, the army could no longer function properly, and implying that if denied, any further disaster to the army could not be blamed on him.

By 11:00 A.M. on the 1st, Pope was confident in his belief of Jackson's advance down the pike, and now prepared his own plan of defense, with no indication at all of renewing an attack. His sense of doom and defeatism still permeated his wires to Washington. He told Halleck in his cable of that hour that the Confederates were advancing on Fairfax down the Little River Turnpike and that he would be forced to attack their advance "once his movement is sufficiently developed." He also warned Halleck that he should "make all preparations for a vigorous defense of the entrenchments around Washington" because Pope was convinced that "I have nothing like the force you undoubtedly suppose."[18]

Apparently determined to make at least a last stand near Fairfax, Pope was now fully concentrating on his Germantown buildup. His greatest ally, ironically, at this point was the napping Jackson, whose midday stop at Chantilly allowed the Union strengthening to continue unimpeded.

At noon on the first, Pope fired off an order to Irvin McDowell to "march rapidly back to Fairfax Court House with your whole *division* [*sic*], assume command of the two brigades now there [Torbert and Hinks] , and immediately occupy Germantown with your whole force, so as to cover the turnpike from this place to Alexandria. Jackson is reported advancing on Fairfax with 20,000 men. Move quickly."[19]

Then at 1 P.M., Pope reversed himself and put General Joseph Hooker, a division commander in Samuel Heintzelman's III Corps, in command of the defenses at Germantown, in lieu of Irvin McDowell. Pope's motives in this change of command are unknown, but it should be apparent that his confidence in McDowell was lacking. In addition, any exchange of words between Generals McDowell and Hooker that may have occurred regarding their respective orders do not survive on the record. Despite Hooker's previous wire to Pope that his troops were ill-prepared for another engagement, he was given command. McDowell's reputation had plummeted so low due to his actions at Second Manassas, that as word spread of this change in command, and the troops passed Hooker proudly mounted on his white stallion, cheers erupted even amongst McDowell's own men.[20]

On his way there along the Warrenton Turnpike, Hooker met up with General Marsena Patrick's brigade from McDowell's Corps, that was now in quick march back to Germantown, per Pope's orders. Advancing up the Little River Pike from Germantown, the brigade struck off to the left of the road and formed their line of battle in old rebel rifle pits just west of the village. With the narrow valley of the Difficult Run before them, they hunkered down for the remainder of the day to await the enemy's advance.[21]

Galloping on, Hooker came across the 1st Rhode Island Cavalry. The Rhode Island troopers were in bivouac near Fairfax Court House and had just settled down to their first hot meal in days when the "boots and saddles" bugle call sounded. Forced hastily to abandon their stew, the grumbling cavalrymen mounted their horses and quickly trotted north about one and a half miles to the Germantown area in a four abreast column astride the Little River Turnpike. Their orders were to feel out the Confederate positions, since according to Hooker, "the enemy was making an attempt to get between us and Washington."[22] Marsena Patrick's 80th New York had also been ordered to return to Centreville when it ran into Hooker along the Warrenton Turnpike. Like the Rhode Islanders, he ordered them, at approximately 3 P.M., to return to Germantown and then advance up the Little River Turnpike where they discovered the old earthworks that had been built by the Confederates the prior winter at the junction of the Little River Turnpike and the Flint Hill Road.[23]

Orders soon came from Hooker for them to advance up the left side of the pike and to hold the woods near Difficult Run "at all hazards." At this point elements of Fitz Lee's Confederate cavalry brigade (under Jeb Stuart) were attempting to make their way down the pike from Ox Hill to clear it out for Jackson's hoped-for advance.[24] Major John Pelham, commanding a section of Stuart's horse artillery, brought up a mountain howitzer that had been situated near the pike to fire grape and canister at the Federals. The hurried Confederates swiftly set up the piece within two hundred yards of the Union skirmishers, but they soon retired for the day after their gunners started being picked off by the Northern marksmen. Soon after, a second cannon launching solid shot opened up on the Federals from farther up the pike with little effect. Other than these brief exchanges, rebel artillery would not be involved in the Ox Hill fight.[25]

Elements of Starke's division also arrived as a skirmish line for assistance, prompting the rebel troopers to trot off out of the way to their extreme left. The rattle of musket fire commenced then and there with Union skirmishers and Lee's dismounted cavalry for about two hours. In the words of a Rhode Island cavalryman, "Here again the metallic shower poured down furiously upon us." After losing two horses and having two men wounded, they retired back to their entrenchments, where they were warmly greeted by the 2nd Rhode Island Infantry.[26]

Jeb Stuart later reported that it was "plainly indicated that the enemy would here make a stand" and that further offensive action was not forthcoming.[27] At this point the Confederate flanking attempt was, for all practical purposes, halted by several Federal infantry and cavalry regiments, due in large measure to the impending clash south of Ox Hill, which would soon occupy the Confederates' full attention.

Jackson's unusual lethargy in the handling of his men on this day can be debated, but his true intentions will be forever shrouded. He had the options of a head-on assault on the position at Germantown, or a quick strike south down the Ox Road to intercept the retreating Federals on the Warrenton Pike. This latter option posed the obvious dangers of then being hit on both flanks. Pope's forces at Centreville could smash into his right while the ever-increasing Germantown forces could move out and slam into his new left flank, crushing his line in between. Jackson chose to do neither, opting instead for a several hour rest at Ox Hill. If he was planning either move, his hand was to be forced before he was ready by Union actions later in the day.

Pope had been strengthening his position at Germantown and, in the end, was going to make sure that if Jackson attacked the Union entrenchments along the Little River Turnpike and at Germantown there would be hell to pay. By mid-afternoon, Irvin McDowell had his entire corps back at Germantown, with General James Ricketts' entire second division drawn up in line of battle awaiting Jackson's advance.[28] That advance would not occur, for Jackson had been ordered by Lee to fight only on the most generous of terms, and while he little feared the Union troops in his front leaving their entrenchments to attack, he was not going to assault them head-on either. Instead he would wait for Lee and Longstreet to catch up to him, then it could be decided what to do next. Heros von Borcke, a German-born giant of a man who was a key aide to Stuart, and present with the cavalier during his two meetings with Jackson on the 1st, noted in his memoir that the Confederate leaders "did not suppose that they [the Federals] really intended to make a stand at that point, and their further retreat to Alexandria was fully expected." According to von Borcke, even Lee "did not deem it advisable to press them vigorously the day after the battle at Groveton."[29] It can therefore be surmised that the usually aggressive Jackson, no doubt as physically exhausted as his men, opted for a *planned* waiting strategy if his way was not *easily* obtained, per orders from Lee, and that his midday nap was not as derelict as it may have first appeared.

The sounds of the skirmishing along the Little River Turnpike brought Jeb Stuart and Jackson galloping to the front along the eastern slope of Ox Hill. Surveying the escalating action, Stonewall ordered Stuart to ascertain if the bluecoats were only making a demonstration, or if a general advance was under way.[30] Clearly frustrated in his attempts to drive the Yankees off the Little River Pike, Stuart rode with Fitzhugh Lee's cavalry brigade about three miles in a north-northeast direction from Ox Hill toward Flint Hill *(modern-day Oakton)* in an attempt to circle around, assess, and possibly attack the Union right flank. This second attempt of Stuart's to clear the pike for Jackson played out no better than the first. The Union line was well covered and any attempt by Stuart's troopers to slice through was unsuccessful. For Stuart, it was clear that the Federals had their flank fully covered. With the way at Flint Hill blocked, darkness at hand, and then hearing in his rear the outbreak of what was quickly becoming the main battle at Chantilly, Stuart turned his force around and galloped back toward Ox Hill.[31]

No doubt in a foul mood on their ride back to Ox Hill, Stuart's troopers ran into a small band of civilians who had been heading west to their farms after taking refuge at the Flint Hill home of James L. Smith. Any able-bodied civilian male in northern Virginia was considered a Union loyalist as those with Southern sympathies were already in Confederate service, therefore they were promptly taken prisoner by the rebel horsemen. Smith's daughter wrote years later, "They all came by home but Father was not permitted to come to the house. He called, 'Frances, I'm going—goodbye!' and mother

answered, 'James, Goodbye'. Did I cry? No. Mother forestalled anything like that by saying, 'Charlotte, don't you dare to cry. It will only
please the Rebels more.'" Smith would spend two months at the
Confederate's Libby Prison in Richmond before being traded for a
prominent rebel citizen of Fairfax.[32] As in all wars, civilian casualties
were inevitable and often the hardest.

━━━━━━━

Several hours earlier, back at his post near Centreville, General Fitz John Porter, commander of the Union V Corps and confidant of General George McClellan had sent prophetic, worried words
to the general in Washington: "Bayard reports the enemy forming in
on the Chantilly road, and my pickets that they are coming down the
Little River turnpike. Twelve brass guns were seen, and infantry and
cavalry. I can see the dust and flags....I think we will have a fight
before night. The enemy are between us and Fairfax Court-House,
and shelled our trains last night. We will fight, or they will avoid us
and strike our rear first. We have been held on thirty-six hours too
long....God speed your operations, and enable you and others in
authority to save our country."[33]

"That hat will be the death of him" 4

Late Afternoon and Early Evening—September 1, 1862

The IX Corps Moves Out

To strengthen further the retreat from Centreville to Fairfax, and to slow Jackson and his advancing rebels, Pope ordered the IX Corps, under the command of thirty-nine-year-old Major General Jesse L. Reno to march hastily eastward along the Warrenton Turnpike and then turn north, marching across fields, where Reno's men would then intercept the Confederate advance by taking and securing the Little River Turnpike at a point some two miles east of Chantilly. Like Jackson, Reno was a graduate of the distinguished 1846 West Point class that also included George

General Jesse L. Reno
Massachusetts MOLLUS, USAMHI

McClellan and Confederate General George Pickett. Now for the third time in a two-week period, these two old friends and western Virginians by birth were about to square off against each other.[1] Since Reno had recently fallen ill with an unreported ailment that was severe enough to keep him off active duty, leadership was given to General Isaac Stevens of the 1st Division.[2] His staff and other

47

officers, morose and dejected after their defeat at Second Manassas, had anxiously looked forward to a badly needed day of rest after the bitter fighting at Bull Run. One-half of the division had been some type of casualty in the past week such that only 2,012 muskets were counted as ready that morning, so Stevens probably sensed what was coming when the marching orders arrived. His exhausted brigades had been pulling rear guard duty the previous day when they were finally relieved the night of the 31st from their rain-soaked position amongst hills and heavy woods overlooking Cub Run, just west of Centreville, by the division of Union General John Reynolds. For a while, the two men heatedly debated the merits of Stevens' position. Reynolds was adamant that the rebels would strike again at any moment, for his men had been shot at while taking their posts, but Stevens nevertheless did not see a full-scale attack as forthcoming. "I think it most probable that the enemy will move around and strike us under the ribs," was his firmly stated conviction.[3]

Fortunately for the Federals, two excited cavalrymen who had been out foraging for their horses had seen the Confederate column moving down the pike. Quickly pounding their way to Pope's headquarters with the news, the riders were then dispatched to Stevens' division where they arrived around 1:00 P.M., with orders from Pope to serve as guides. Pope's orders for Stevens were that he was to march immediately across country to the Little River Turnpike. At that point he was to take a position across the road and hold in check the enemy who was purportedly advancing down the pike.[4]

Stevens wasted no time in giving the order for his regiments to fall in, understanding full well the danger to the Yankee retreat that loomed. Camp rumors had been rampant throughout the day of impending marches, yet nothing had been forthcoming, so many troops viewed this order as just the latest false alarm, causing many lackadaisically to take their places in line with filled coffee cups still in hand.[5] Stevens quickly moved his men out of bivouac and set out immediately with his division in the lead and Reno's 2nd Division following.[6] By 4:30 Pope had all his corps responding and on the march. General Samuel Heintzelman's III Corps was dispatched with orders to follow the IX Corps and assist if need be. Pope then wired McDowell, who was now in Germantown, at 4:00 P.M.: "If you hear a battle raging to-night near Centreville advance to the north, keeping your communication open with Reno and near to him, also by the right with Hooker, who will advance his left to your right."[7] Since

McDowell would have needed to move west rather than north, coupled with the fact that the skirmishing was under way when received, this latest confusing wire ultimately served no purpose.

After marching about two and one-half miles from the Union encampments on Centreville heights, Stevens took his troops off the Warrenton Pike, veering to his left. He led his men onto a narrow cart path heading in a north-easterly direction with the 79th New York "Highlanders," Stevens' old regimental command at the head. The Highlanders were men of Scottish descent who were known for their parade dress of Scottish kilts and headgear, though it is doubtful if this attire was ever worn in battle. The column emerged on an elevated knoll several hundred yards west of the Milan house, which had been the residence of the War of 1812 hero John Milan. From this vantage, the ground sloped downward toward the edges of Difficult Run, near the depression of the then-unfinished Manassas railroad, an extension of the same embankment used so suc-

**Fatigue uniform and kilts
of the 79th New York**

Battles and Leaders

cessfully by Jackson at Manassas three days earlier, and then up toward an open field where the Reid family home and farm could be seen. Just behind the Reid house to the northwest was a thirty-acre field of small, stunted corn.[8] The cornfield sloped slightly upward and terminated into dense woods on the field's left and to the front, with a thin snake-rail fence separating the two. About three hundred yards beyond the initial northern tree line lay the Little River Turnpike and the Confederate main body. To the right of the cornfield, and of roughly similar size lay an open grassy plain, probably used for grazing purposes, whose right side ended at the Ox Road *(modern Route 608 aka West Ox Road).* Nestled between the two fields

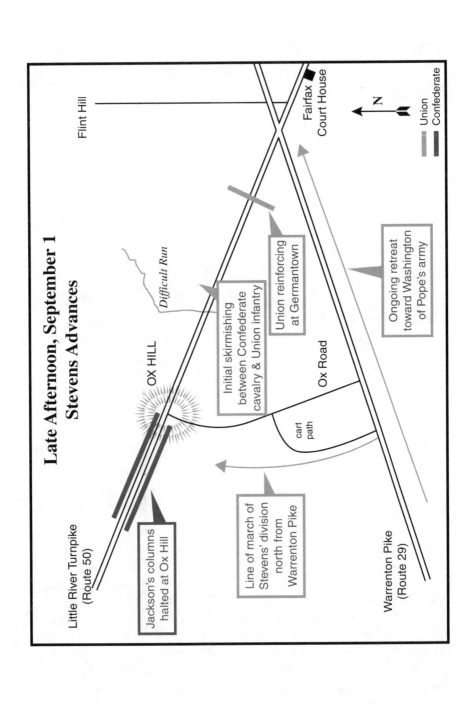

Late Afternoon, September 1
Stevens Advances

Flint Hill

Little River Turnpike
(Route 50)

Difficult Run

OX HILL

Jackson's columns
halted at Ox Hill

Initial skirmishing
between Confederate
cavalry & Union infantry

Union reinforcing
at Germantown

cart
path

Ox Road

Line of march of
Stevens' division
north from
Warrenton Pike

Ongoing retreat
toward Washington
of Pope's army

Warrenton Pike
(Route 29)

Fairfax
Court House

N

Union
Confederate

at the southern edge immediately behind the Reid house was a small apple orchard.

General Stevens' shocked gaze beheld in the distance an entire line of rebel skirmishers emerging from the distant tree line and advancing across the plain. Stevens was without orders to attack, but he surmised that if he was to accomplish his primary mission of getting to and then blocking the Little River Turnpike, he would have to deal with this skirmish line which he also rightly believed was the precursor of a larger force close behind. In retrospect, we know that Stevens beat Jackson to the punch, that Jackson was waiting for Lee and Longstreet to come up, and had no intention at this point of attacking to his south. Stevens, of course, would not have known this at the time, and assumed that the skirmish line was the initial force driving south to cut off the Federal retreat. If Stevens was to prevent that move south, or move his men to the north-northeast to gain the turnpike, then his only option was to go forward and attack.

General Jesse Reno, still ailing, had now arrived on the scene with his 2nd Division and conversed with Stevens on the situation. Reno appeared undecided and hesitating, though it is not known what words passed between them. But it is known that Reno did not overrule Stevens' tactical analysis and plan, leaving field command to Stevens. The ailing Reno would be content to act as field supervisor of the various deployments.[9] Shortly thereafter, Reno sent his 2nd Brigade under Colonel Edward Ferrero to the right of the Ox Road for support, while Reno's remaining brigade under Colonel James Nagle (6th and 9th New Hampshire, 2nd Maryland, and 48th Pennsylvania) was initially held back in reserve.

**Colonel Edward Ferrero,
51st New York Infantry**

USAMHI

With the skies continuing to darken portentously, and the wind beginning to strengthen, the general began assembling his men in battle
formation, and sent the division's provost marshal racing back to
Heintzelman to report the pending engagement and request immediate support.[10]

The Battle Commences

Stevens' men had been marching in column and were quickly
given the order to form battle lines at the double-quick. That forced
the back regiments to run a good distance to their points in the line.
Before advancing, they were given a few minutes to catch their collective breaths. Private Rice of the 50th Pennsylvania sadly recalled
a fellow warrior who huffed into line saying, "I'm a little short winded
boys, but when I do get there, I can shoot as well as any of you." In
a few minutes he would be among the first to fall, without ever firing
a shot.[11]

Stevens had his battle column arranged as follows: the first line
had the 79th New York on the right with the 28th Massachusetts on
their left. The second line had the 8th Michigan on the right with the
50th Pennsylvania to their left. The third and final line consisted of
the 46th New York on the right with the 100th Pennsylvania to their
left. Three companies of the 79th New York deployed in front as
skirmishers, and then the entire division began advancing steadily
down the slope toward the rebel skirmish line near the old railroad
bed, just as General Jesse Reno arrived with George Durell's Pennsylvania battery. Members of the 100th Pennsylvania "Roundhead"
regiment debated amongst themselves as they advanced as to
whether the line of men they saw off in the distance were "Unionists
or Johnnies," but all doubt was cast aside when they made out the
"old white blanket in a roll across the shoulder."[12]

The initial shots rang out, alerting all of an engagement getting
under way. Confederate marksmen hiding in trees or behind the rise
quickly began playing havoc with the advance bluecoats from Company K of the front-line 28th Massachusetts. The men paused and
started ducking as bullets whizzed around them, prompting their still-
unaware Captain Brennan to frustratingly cry out, "What the hell are
you bobbing your heads for?" A moment latter, a rebel minié ball
crashed into his field glasses, dropping him to his knees. The Bay
Staters began to return the fire, causing the hidden rebels to withdraw.[13] As the rebel skirmish line began slowly to back off, Isaac

Stevens and staff dismounted their horses and ordered his division forward at the double-quick. With two of his three brigade commanders out of action due to serious wounds suffered at Second Bull Run, Stevens decided he was going to lead this advance personally.[14]

The Confederates Set Up

It is not known if Stonewall was awakened from his nap by his skirmishers' reports of a sizable Union force approaching from the south, but because of this news Stonewall now knew that Federal forces were fully aware of his location and intent. Not yet wanting a general engagement, but realizing one was about to occur, Jackson ordered light division commander A. P. Hill to send the North Carolina brigade of General Lawrence O' Bryan Branch, and the Virginia brigade of Colonel Charles Field, to march south from the Little River Turnpike to find out what he was up against.[15] Since Field had also been wounded at Second Manassas, his men were now under the command of thirty-two-year-old Colonel John M. Brockenbrough of

**Confederate Colonel
John M. Brockenbrough,
a post-war image**

He commanded "Field's Brigade" at Ox Hill.

USAMHI

**Confederate General
Lawrence O'Bryan Branch**

Miller, *Photographic History of the Civil War*

the 40th Virginia Infantry. The skirmish line that Stevens witnessed was from these brigades. The main body of the two brigades began to double-quick through the woods to meet the enemy they knew would be waiting. When the sound of battle and the skirmishers' reports got back to "Ol' Jack," he hurriedly rushed the deployment of the remainder of his corps. His old "Stonewall Brigade" was sent to anchor the far left of the Confederate line in an almost perpendicular position to the Little River Turnpike just east of Ox Hill and at its base. General Alexander Lawton's division was deployed in the middle, forming an arc up and over the Ox Hill ridgeline between the Ox Road and the turnpike. His division included Hays' Louisiana brigade, now commanded by Colonel Henry Strong, which was placed along the snake rail fence at the woods' western edge. A. P. Hill's division with its six infantry regiments anchored the right side of the Confederate line.

The Charge

On down the slope Stevens' division advanced, past the never-to-be finished Manassas Railroad bed and on up the incline. When they finally reached the Reid farmhouse, they were met by the elderly residents who shouted without hesitation, "We haven't seen any Southern soldiers about here at all, and we hope there won't be any fighting about the house!" Several shots then rang out, hitting two of the Highlanders, which put an end to all conversation with the residents of the farmhouse. The Union soldiers sprinted forward seeking the cover of the apple orchard. They were ordered to continue the advance through the cornfield, however many men were famished, and the temptation to fill their haversacks with the fruit was great. Between shots, some men began to shake the trees, hoping to bring down some of the apples. Unfortunately, noted one of the men, "we found that shaking the trees brought more than fruit; it told the enemy, who were posted on higher ground, just where we were, and their bullets rained into the orchard, severing twigs and bringing down as many apples as we cared to pick up."[16]

Some Confederate skirmishers simply stood in awe and watched while the two armies formed their battle lines, while the main body of Branch's and Brockenbrough's brigades arrived at the edge of the woods. When the Union troops were within 150 yards, the rebel skirmishers fired. After two rounds from the skirmishers the main line of Confederates at the woods emerged and began to advance

The Confederates Set Their Line

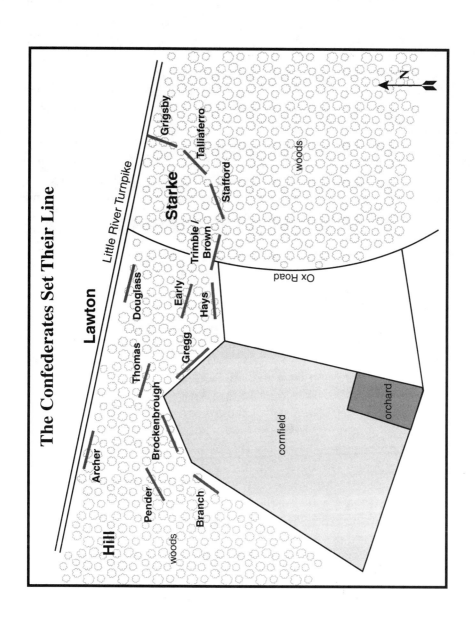

rapidly in battle line formation. Into the cornfield they pressed. One Confederate skirmisher recalled how he had hoped to stay there and watch the intensifying fight, but he was forced to rapidly run about twenty yards to the safety of a tree, bullets cutting his clothes as he ran.[17]

Ordered to support the Union advance, the Massachusetts artillery battery of Lieutenant Samuel Benjamin rushed up the Ox Road and onto a knoll near the Milan house, about four hundred yards from the Confederate-occupied woods. From there the guns opened on the Confederates with some accuracy, slowly driving the rebel skirmish line back into the trees.[18]

The rebel line slowly but steadily retired and finally disappeared into the trees. Not a single rebel soldier remained in sight. To many bluecoats, it now seemed as if they had never been there at all. Stevens' column continued to advance in fine fashion, bayonets gleaming in the diminishing daylight. Nothing lay in front but open field, at a slight incline, extending over two hundred yards to their front with the wall of woods closing the field in on three sides. At the edge of the tree line ran an old snake rail fence. With the Federals advancing, the troops of Branch's brigade waited on the northwestern edge of the cornfield. Brockenbrough's brigade at the northern end, while Hays' Louisiana brigade had been brought up at the woods' edge facing the open field in front. Here they silently crouched behind the fence, muskets cocked and ready, and waited for the advancing Union line. Coming out of the woods on their left, and formed in front of the grassy field, General Isaac Trimble's brigade line extended across the Ox Road and continued just into the woods east of there. One of Trimble's men from the 15th Alabama remembered: "We had not gone far before we met our skirmishers in retreat, closely pursued by the Yankees...We were in a thick body of woods, so thick that we could only see a few yards in front, but the hissing bullets from the enemy as they came rapping the bushes and trees, and occasionally hitting a man, was evidence to us that they were not far away."[19]

"There is no enemy there!" exclaimed Captain William Lusk of the 79th New York as he marched with Captain Hazard Stevens, son of the general. "They have fallen back, we shall find nothing there."[20] The captain could not have been more wrong and soon

Early 1900s view of the Chantilly battlefield from near the Confederate line looking south

The Reid house is faintly visible at the far right. Stevens' men would have advanced from the background toward the camera. Today, the entire view would be filled with commercial development.

realized the severity of his mistake. At that very moment, Strong's Louisianans, who were crouched at the tree line let loose with a volley that staggered the 79th New York, and was then rippled along the entire front line. Captain Hazard Stevens of the 79th was among those severely injured. When asked a few moments later if he was aware of his son's wounding, General Isaac Stevens replied that he was, but realizing that delay was not an option, he ordered the line forward again, this time slanting a bit to the left.[21] Recovering a semblance of order, the bluecoats began to return the fire. Noting the extent of the rebel line in front of him, Stevens brought up his second line, and then finally the third, including the 100th Pennsylvania, affectionately known as the "Roundheads," and shouted out the order, "Five companies of the Roundheads for skirmishers!" prolonging the line to the left of the 79th New York "Highlanders."[22] Stevens' division was now under a withering fire from the somewhat hidden Confederates, who had swung out on his left flank and delivered a galling fire. Private Rice remembered, "Their bullets came among us like rain, our men falling thick and fast at every step."[23] All along the line officers were yelling and exhorting their men to continue. Even the regimental chaplain of the 100th "Roundheads" was in the thick of it with his men, shouting, "Boys, remember Cromwell! Trust in God and keep your powder dry!" The Federal line paused at the base of the hill, returning fire with everything they had.[24] Unfortunately for the bluecoats, they were totally exposed to the rebel sharpshooters at the edge of the woods.

The line had now stalled, seemingly unable or unwilling to continue. Realizing that his men were in a precarious position, Stevens knew the attack had to continue or a massacre of his men would occur on that very spot. He also knew that support was desperately needed or his men were likewise doomed. Lieutenant Horatio Belcher, aide to Stevens, had been ordered just before the advance began to gallop back to the Warrenton Pike with all possible haste and seek reinforcements. A number of the first officers he reached refused to assist, claiming they could not advance without higher orders to do so, but his luck changed upon reaching General Philip Kearny, First Division commander of the III Corps, Army of the Potomac. Kearny's men were also known as the "Red Patch Division," because of the identifying red patch each man was required to wear on his hat or cap, in order to establish esprit de corps through a unique identifying mark.

"By damn!, I'll support Stevens anywhere!" was the general's unhesitating reply. Kearny had always held a deep respect for Stevens, not to mention that his division's current duty was to support the Army of the Potomac's IX Corps.[25] He wasted no time in putting his men into motion.

Earlier that morning, III Corps commander Major General Samuel Heintzelman had moved his camp an additional mile to the east to form a reserve for Sumner's Corps, as ordered. At 1:00 P.M., Heintzelman and Sumner were ordered to march their men at daylight the next morning across the Little River Turnpike in the direction of Chantilly, to assist in the defense against what was still believed to be only a developing rebel threat. Heintzelman had just returned to his headquarters and given the necessary orders when he received a vital notice from Pope that the Confederates were about to attack, and to get his corps under arms with all possible haste. By 3:30 P.M., he was ordered to fall back on the Warrenton Pike toward Fairfax Court House about two and one-half miles and face to the north, in order to aid Reno's IX Corps. By 4:00 P.M., Heintzelman and Kearny's First Division were on the march.[26] Joseph Hooker's division, under the temporary command of General Cuvier Grover, followed close behind.

Kearny immediately diverted General David Birney's Second Brigade, III Army Corps, off the Warrenton Turnpike and north up the Ox Road toward the unmistakable clatter of musketry.[27] Concurrently, Kearny placed General John C. Robinson's First Brigade in a line of battle just west of the Centreville Road, along with Captain William Graham's battery of the 1st U.S. artillery. As far as Kearny could tell, most of the rebel army was still off to the north and west of his current position, so he knew Birney's left flank had to be protected. Robinson's brigade faced to the northwest and consisted of the 63rd and 105th Pennsylvania Infantry regiments, plus the 20th Indiana, which was on high ground holding the woods to the right of their line. The brigade's line was about one-half mile from the Warrenton Pike. Kearny's third, and final, brigade, commanded by Colonel Orlando M. Poe, was ordered to form in line of battle on the Warrenton Pike and move forward in the direction of the firing then going on between Stevens' division and the enemy, until their left fully connected with General Robinson's right.[28]

As with their Confederate brethren, there was always time for a bit of gallows humor when on the march, as one of Birney's New Yorkers later evoked. "As I started watching the 40th 'Mozart regiment' go by, I had my double barreled shotgun in my hand which caused many of my old regiment to jeer—asking me to go with them and shoot rabbits for them, while they shot 'Johnnies' (or Rebels)."[29]

The intense Confederate fire had taken its toll on the front Union line. Five color bearers of the 79th New York had fallen in a span of only twenty minutes.[30] Stevens was now becoming aware that his right flank urgently needed reinforcements as well. Hastily commanding his orders, the request for immediate support was rushed back to Reno.[31] Realizing that the need for decisive action was at hand, the diminutive 5'1" Isaac Stevens decided to rush to the front line and lead his men forward personally in a last ditch charge. In one of the more poignant images of Civil War lore, Stevens grabbed the colors of his beloved 79th New York "Highlanders" from the wounded color bearer. Ignoring the wounded man's plea of, "For God's sake, don't take the colors, general; they'll shoot you if you do!" Stevens quickly retorted, "Give me the colors! If they don't follow me now, they never will!" and then cried over the din of musketry and artillery

Confederate line in the woods

Battles and Leaders

to his troops, "Highlanders, my Highlanders, follow your general!"[32] The proud Irishmen of the 28th Massachusetts, also in the front line with the 79th New York, joined in gallantly, and with colors held high, Stevens led the attacking regiments up the now fairly steep incline[33] and over the fence, then into the tree line where the rebel line was quickly beginning to break. Stevens' other regiments quickly followed suit as best they could. Lieutenant Belcher of the 8th Michigan, having returned from reaching Kearny, later recalled, "We advanced steadily amidst a perfect hail of lead till we drove them back and entered the woods ourselves thus getting on equal footing with them."[34]

Union General Isaac Ingalls Stevens
The hero of Ox Hill

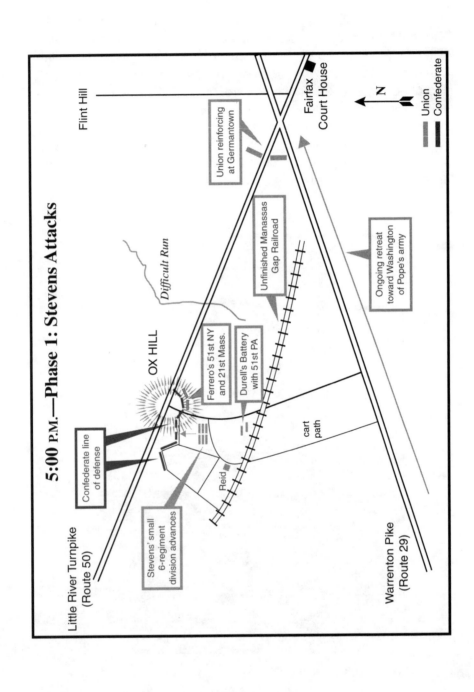

5:00 P.M.—Phase 1: Stevens Attacks

Little River Turnpike
(Route 50)

Flint Hill

Difficult Run

OX HILL

Confederate line
of defense

Stevens' small
6-regiment
division advances

Ferrero's 51st NY
and 21st Mass.

Durell's Battery
with 51st PA

Reid

cart
path

Unfinished Manassas
Gap Railroad

Union reinforcing
at Germantown

Ongoing retreat
toward Washington
of Pope's army

Fairfax
Court House

Warrenton Pike
(Route 29)

N

Union
Confederate

Then, at the moment of his greatest military glory, Stevens fell dead instantly, the victim of a rebel bullet that entered his temple. He fell to the ground, flagstaff still in hand, his much-loved flag slowly draping his body.[35] His death would prove decisive to his division and, sadly, had been eerily predicted by Union artillerist Samuel Benjamin, who spoke to the general just prior to the advance. "I saw him going up to the wood near his line, with his little panama hat on, the ground to our right having not been cleared, and I said to [the] 'Lord, that hat will be the death of him, the sharpshooters will hit him in the head.' In a minute after I heard he was dead."[36] The general's wish for a warrior's death had come to pass, for several men of the 79th New York later suggested that Stevens had said in the past that if he was to be killed in battle, he hoped it would be a clean shot through the temple.

With the passing of Stevens, command of the division fell on the shoulders of Colonel Benjamin C. Christ of the 50th Pennsylvania, the lone brigade commander still unscathed from the previous three days' worth of fighting. Though their general had fallen, the 79th surged forward into the woods, as Hays' Louisiana brigade began to crumble before them.

At the first rush, regiment commander Major William Monaghan of the 6th Louisiana fell wounded, creating confusion in the front of the line where he was positioned. The uncertain rebels began to fall back not only due to this loss, but also because of an untimely and ill-conceived move by Colonel Henry B. Strong, a forty-one-year-old Irishman who was the brigade's third commander in less than four months, and had held that distinction for only three days. The prior commander, Colonel Henry Forno, had been wounded on August 30 at Second Manassas, while the unit's namesake, General Harry Hays, had yet to return to the brigade due to a serious shoulder wound suffered at Port Republic on June 8, 1862.[37]

Fellow brigade commander, General Jubal Early, later sternly alleged that Strong's "want of sufficient skill in the command of a brigade caused him to get confused," since Strong had attempted to realign his regiments at the last moment leaving no organized front to oppose the 79th's charge when it came at them.[38] Lieutenant George Ring of the 6th Louisiana, who was personally engaged in the melee, vehemently disagreed in his diary with the general. Ring instead placed responsibility on division commander General Alexander Lawton for failing to send forward adequate support, writing: "Our division being badly handled, our brigade had to bear the brunt of the battle unsupported for two hours. Our regiment after fighting against desperate odds for two hours fell back in confusion after Major Monaghan was wounded."[39]

Colonel Henry B. Strong

He commanded "Hays' Brigade" at Ox Hill. This is the only known image.
Courtesy of James Gannon, *Irish Rebels, Confederate Tigers*

The initial break continued to the left affecting as well elements of Trimble's brigade, who were positioned astride the Ox Road. William Oates of the 15th Alabama, and of later Little Round Top fame, recalled: "[division commander A. P.] Hill's brigades were driven back, and the Louisiana brigade gave way, something it had never done before, on any field...Colonel Strong, its commander, doubtless brave enough, was of a very excitable manner, which always has a very demoralizing effect upon the best soldiers. As the Louisiana brigade gave way, one regiment after another of Trimble's brigade followed the example. The 15th Alabama was on the right, Captain I. B. Feagin commanding, and hence was the last to receive the panic. I was acting as major, hence on the left. The 12th was next on the left, and when it began to give way, I tried to stop the men and make them return to the fence. I appealed to the proud record the regiment had previously made, but it was unavailing. An appeal to the pride of men when panic stricken is completely thrown away."[40] Oates' fearful experience was duplicated all along the line and as far back as the turnpike, where Lawton's old Georgia brigade had been placed as support, and were now under the command of thirty-one-year-old Colonel Marcellus Douglass. To the Georgian's surprise, one man was instantly killed and ten wounded from Yankee sharpshooters coming through the woods before return fire halted the bluecoat advance.[41] Captain William Colston of Starke's 2nd Virginia saw panicked men fleeing as far as his position on the far left of the rebel line. "I saw a soldier behind a tree and ran to him and ordered him to go to the front; he stepped back and pointing his gun at me, swore he would not budge. He had the drop on me and I had to let him alone, especially as I saw he belonged to another regiment and brigade."[42]

Like Ewell and Taliaferro before him, General Isaac Trimble had fallen with a severe leg wound at Second Manassas and was out of commission. Now, Trimble's brigade was being commanded by Captain William F. Brown of the 12th Georgia Infantry, which had been transferred into Trimble's brigade just five days earlier. Brown was the senior officer in the brigade and a grizzled veteran whose age was said to be at least sixty years. The much admired old-timer had been recommended for promotion by General Jubal Early following his energetic feats a month earlier at Cedar Mountain.[43] Now the large-built man with his trademark black plume waving in his hat was frantically trying to duplicate that earlier performance. The Georgian's line was breaking and he was doing everything in his power to stop it, racing along the line, cursing and imploring his men to stand and fight. Brown's face was aglow with rage as he waved his sabre at the approaching Federals. Like Isaac Stevens before him a few minutes earlier, he was struck in the head by an enemy minié ball and killed instantly. Brown would be the only Confederate brigade commander killed at Ox Hill, and his death would continue the decimation amongst the ranks of Southern military leadership. His replacement would be Colonel James Walker of the 13th Virginia.[44]

**Captain William F. Brown,
12th Georgia Infantry**

He was killed in action while in command of Trimble's brigade at Ox Hill.

History of the Doles-Cook Brigade

Confederate Line Briefly Breaks

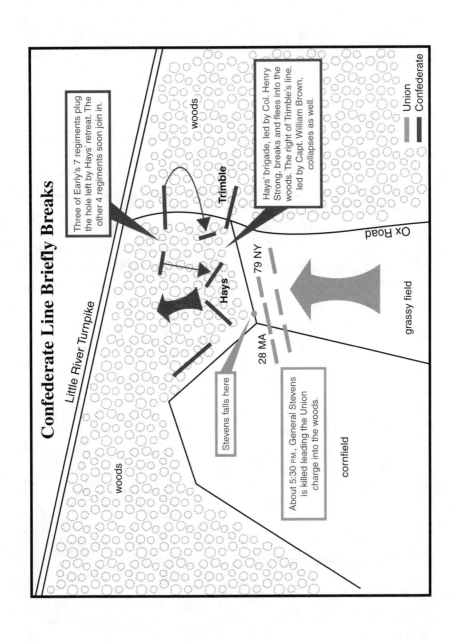

Three of Early's 7 regiments plug the hole left by Hays' retreat. The other 4 regiments soon join in.

Hays' brigade, led by Col. Henry Strong, breaks and flees into the woods. The right of Trimble's line, led by Capt. William Brown, collapses as well.

Trimble

Hays

woods

Little River Turnpike

woods

Ox Road

79 NY

28 MA

Stevens falls here

About 5:30 P.M., General Stevens is killed leading the Union charge into the woods.

grassy field

cornfield

Union
Confederate

Fortunately for Strong's Louisianans, as well as Trimble's brigade, elements of Jubal Early's Virginia brigade were moving behind them at that very moment to the far left of the Confederate line. They were to confront what General William Starke feared to be a large formation of Federal troops forming near a gap between the turnpike and the Confederate far left. Early had been reluctant to move without orders, but relented when he reconnoitered the ground and saw Starke's panicked state. In truth, Starke's worry was understandable and perhaps predictable. The forty-

General William E. Starke

His division anchored the left side of the Confederate line.

Library of Congress

eight-year-old Starke had been promoted to brigadier general only three weeks earlier and now, because of mounting losses to the Confederate senior command, was facing an early attempt at divisional command. As the far left of the Confederate arced line, elements of his division were now facing east, at a ninety degree angle to the Little River Turnpike. They had already provided the troops for the heavy skirmishing to their front down in the Difficult Run valley. His men were stationed in heavy woods plus their sight was further diminished with the naturally approaching dusk and unusually overcast skies. With the heavy fighting off to his right (south) at full tempo, Starke had every reason to assume he was about to get hit on two fronts. However, three regiments of Early's brigade, the 13th, 25th, and 31st Virginia, had gotten separated in the woods from the rest of the brigade during the march to their left. When General Early sent Lieutenant Sam Early (the general's brother) back to see what had happened, he quickly learned that his missing three regiments had fortuitously ended up plugging the hole created by the breaking of Strong's confused Louisianans.[45] One Virginian who helped stem the Union rush into the trees remembered: "...the Yanks came within twenty steps of us before they saw us. We fired into them and I tell you they made tracks."[46] Early quickly turned his other four regiments

Confederate General Jubal Early, 1850s image
Virginia Military Institute Archives

around and sent them scurrying back to help secure the line left in limbo by Hays' retreat.

━━━━━━━━━

When Stevens gave his final command to assault the rebel line, the 28th Massachusetts made sure their bayonets were properly fixed and charged along with the 79th New York. One Massachusetts private later wrote of the carnage to his family: "When we got into the woods, we ran through what we did not shoot. We bayoneted them. One man begged and got no mercy, a Yankee ran him through. Thank God it was not an Irishman [that] did it."[47] Due to the heavy weather and the resultant wet gunpowder, the battle at Ox Hill would be one of the rare instances in the Civil War where use of the bayonet was common. The fighting in the woods was intense and often hand-to-hand, but the battered New York and Massachusetts men were slowly being pushed back out of the dense woods by the arrival of Early's fresh troops.

Meanwhile, the disorganized remnants of Hays' Louisianans managed to rally and regroup behind Early's regiments. Division commander Alexander Lawton quickly placed them under Early's command, who then sent them forward to form just to the left of his Virginia brigade. It seemed to be over almost as soon as it started. Early's Virginians had filled the gap properly, forcing the Federals to break off the attack and fall back. Though he admitted that he was not able personally to see the fight through the thick screen of woods, Early later reported that "the enemy had been successfully repulsed by my three regiments."[48] A private in Trimble's 12th Georgia wrote to his wife the next day that the entire melee could not have lasted more than ten minutes.[49]

As this stage of the fighting wound down, Hays' regrouped Louisianans reached their original line at the front, though badly mauled. Over one hundred men had been either killed or wounded in their unfortunate earlier maneuvering. Not all of the rebels had run, however, nor had they all stayed to fight. As the firing continued, Private William Snakenberg of the 14th Louisiana was aggressively loading cartridges into his cartridge box when he was asked by an officer who were the two men huddled under a blanket behind a nearby stump. He was ordered by the officer to see who they were. "I got up and pulled the blanket off them and saw that they were of the Virginia Brigade skulking, not wounded. I got them up in a rather rough way....That was a fight in a battle."[50]

"A Terrific, Horrible, Phantasmagoria"

About the time of Stevens' death, generally considered to be around 5:00 P.M., the skies that had been ominously darkening all afternoon finally let loose. The thick, blackened clouds caused an early and unnatural dimness to settle over the field. Though it had been overcast and raining consistently for a day and a half, this time an unseasonably hard, wintry downpour and ferocious wind quickly joined forces to present to Billy Yank and Johnny Reb alike a spectacle none who were there ever forgot as long as they lived. Thunder boomed so loud and continuously that it masked the sound of the artillery both on the battlefield and in Centreville, a good three miles away, while many veterans would later recall that it was often impossible to even differentiate the thunder from the cannon.[51] One awestruck Pennsylvanian never forgot the landscape: "What a grand spectacle the Chantilly fight presented! A terrible rain storm with terrific thunder and lightning prevailed during its continuance—this, combined with the booming of the cannon and rattle of musketry, made up a most indescribable scene, outrivaling pandemonium itself. It was a terrific, horrible, phantasmagoria." A mile to the east at the Union's Germantown defenses, a Rhode Islander wrote in his diary that "It rained in torrents, and never in my life ever heard such thunder or saw such lightning. It seemed as if Nature was trying to outdo man in the way of noise, for all the time the cannon roared and muskets rattled while the air was filled with flying missiles."[52] Any soldier found it virtually impossible to take a cartridge from its box and load it into his rifle before it was drenched. The swirling downpour caused vision to become blurry with the Confederates getting the worst of it as the storm was blowing water directly into their faces.[53] So severe was the deluge that twenty miles to the east in Washington, sidewalks and walkways were flooded as pedestrians waded up to their knees in water.[54]

Rush to the Front

With the initial breaking of Hays' Louisiana brigade, Stonewall Jackson knew he had a full-fledged fight on his hands due to the number of rebels fleeing the woods in disorder and streaming down the Little River Pike. Fearing disaster, he threw virtually his whole corps into the fight and at the same time began moving his artillery well back of the action.[55] Jackson's artillerists repeatedly looked for an open knoll where to place the batteries and then get a good line of fire without fear of hitting their own men, but to no avail. A number of the guns ended up parking in the farm yard of Charles Stewart, just west of Ox Hill on the Little River Turnpike.[56]

The brigades of Brigadier Generals William Dorsey Pender and Maxcy Gregg, along with the Georgia brigade commanded by Colonel Edward L. Thomas, were quickly brought up into support on the Confederate right. Pender's North Carolinians were ordered initially to support Brockenbrough's hard-pressed Virginia brigade, but Pender soon realized that after moving his men about seven hundred yards through intensely thick woods his soldiers were on top of their comrades. This error caused his brigade to get out of alignment, resulting in the brigade becoming separated. Two of Pender's regiments ended up off to the left supporting Thomas, while the 16th and 34th ended up a good distance to the right supporting Branch.[57] Gregg's South Carolinians soon appeared to fill a hole between Brockenbrough and Hays at the northeastern edge of the cornfield. The 13th and 14th South Carolina were set up in the front line with Orr's Rifles and the 12th South Carolina supporting them respectively. The musket firing was intense and galling, and the fence in their front soon came tumbling down. The 13th was on the far right of Gregg's brigade when they were ordered to fix bayonets and

Confederate General
Edward L. Thomas—held the
rank of colonel at Ox hill
USAMHI

Confederate General
Maxcy Gregg
USAMHI

prepare for a charge, but it didn't happen. Instead the order was given to begin firing by file. The 1st South Carolina was held back in reserve, but with bullets hotly whistling through the trees all around them, they were forced to lie face down on the ground. The ongoing torrential cloudburst raised the specter of drowning in the mud for a number of them.[58] Thomas' Georgians then followed Gregg's men into the maelstrom, taking a position just west of the Ox Road.[59]

General Jubal Early's Virginia brigade had already surged forward to fill the breach from where Hays' brigade had fallen back, while William Starke's remaining brigades were sent to the left to bolster the line at the Ox Road and into the woods on the Confederate left, filling in between Trimble and Taliaferro's. Jackson's old "Stonewall Brigade" was already set up as the anchor on the extreme left in an almost perpendicular position to the Little River Turnpike. Brigadier General James Archer's brigade was held in reserve on the Confederate right, well within supporting distance of Gregg's and Thomas' brigade.[60] Archer's men were placed on the turnpike about one-quarter mile west of Ox Hill, while Lawton's old Georgia brigade remained in reserve on the rebel left. Once the battle commenced, Jackson took his artillery from the pike and placed it on a bare and commanding rise, about a half-mile to the west of the Ox Hill ridge, but the dense woods again prevented an effective line of sight for his artillerists. The Confederate infantry was going to have to go at it alone in this fight.[61]

The East Side of Ox Road

Around 5:00 P.M., as Stevens' first division was charging the woods on the Union left, the 51st New York and the 21st Massachusetts of Jesse Reno's old 2nd Division, 2nd Brigade, and now commanded by Colonel Edward Ferrero, were advancing up a slight incline into a dense, heavily wooded front on the Union far right, just east of Ox Road and approximately three-tenths of a mile east of Stevens' men. Far to their rear, they were supported by George Durell's Pennsylvania artillery, with the 51st Pennsylvania Infantry regiment bringing up the rear in support of the battery. Having seen the Confederate pickets in the woods in front of Stevens, the two lead regiments had crossed through the unfinished Manassas Railroad bed, over the Ox Road heading in a north-northeasterly direction. Their orders were to attempt to flank the Confederate left and to advance through the woods until they found the enemy. What these two Union regiments were expected to accomplish against Jackson's host was not explained.[62]

With each step up a slight incline, it appeared that maintaining their proper lines was becoming ever more difficult. The onset of dusk and the thick woods caused the 51st New York to wander well off to the right of the 21st, though men of the 21st Massachusetts had mistakenly believed that the New Yorkers were still directly in their front. This erroneous belief prompted Massachusetts officers to caution their men about firing at any troops in their front and therefore believed no need existed to send out skirmishers. The 51st found themselves wallowing in a water-drenched area that was like "a Cyprus swamp on the extreme right where the trees were so thik [*sic*] we could hardly walk and the rain was falling in torrents completely soaking us." Advancing slowly and cautiously, they encountered the advance pickets from Starke's Confederate division who gave the Federals a heavy volley into their ranks, but due to the dense foliage did little if any damage.[63] The 51st returned the rebel fire with a volley of their own, setting the stage for a brief firefight in the darkened woods. With sight almost nonexistent due to the rain

The still extant woods on the eastside of the battlefield
In these woods the 21st Massachusetts lost over one hundred men with a single volley.
Collection of the author

and darkness, Captain Henry Francis later bemoaned that "...we did not know whether we fighting our own men or the enemy."[64] Ultimately, the New Yorkers succeeded in driving in the few pickets of Starke's that they encountered. It would be the only action of the night for the drenched 51st, who then began trying to find their way back out of the thick forest.

Plowing ahead to the left of the New Yorkers, the 21st was still disconnected from the 51st, with the driving rain now adding to the sight difficulties. Private James Stone of the 21st Massachusetts remembered, "It was soon evident that each command had lost all connection with the other, and was advancing no one knew where or why."[65] The intensely thick woods only added to their sight difficulties. A look at the topography today will reveal a thin but obvious north/south ridgeline, which runs all the way to Ox Hill, whose thick forests at the time also served to separate the two regiments. In spite of the dense foliage, the smattering of gunfire and the quickly returning pickets clearly alerted the rebels that enemy forces were coming up the hill at them. They were positioned most advantageously at the crest of the Ox Hill ridgeline so that they commanded a clear view through the forest of the downward sloping hill but were protected by the curve of the rise. With muskets aimed and hammers locked, the gray and butternut-clad Georgians and North Carolinians of Trimble's brigade awaited the unsuspecting Yanks. The drenched Massachusetts soldiers pressed ahead, their line becoming increasingly broken due to the difficult underbrush and fallen logs they encountered. "The men pushed aside the briars and bushes with one hand, and held up the gun with the other (so that) the rain filled almost every barrel with water."[66] In the ongoing tempest, Captain Charles Walcott of the 21st recalled, no doubt with horror: "In a few minutes we came in sight of a body of troops, in dark uniform, and approached until portions of the regiment were within twenty yards of them, when we halted....A few scattered shots came in on our right, to which our answer was 'Cease firing, we're friends.' Then, while most of our poor fellows were standing with their guns at the shoulder, one of the deadliest volleys ever fired rolled upon us from our right and front. In the sudden anguish and despair of the moment the whole regiment seemed to be lying bleeding on the ground, indeed, almost every man who had stood in the more open spaces of the wood did fall...."[67] In a matter of seconds over one hundred men were killed instantly, including two officers, plus five others died later of their wounds. The 21st began to return the fire as best as possible with their shattered remains. Those who had revolvers used them instead, as the downpour rendered most rifles useless, but the rain and darkness offered little opportunity for accuracy or cohesion, so the Bay Staters soon began to stagger out of the wooded death house, west across Ox Road and into the grassy field beyond.[68]

Several post-battle letter writers, all Union, made allegations that the Confederates were clothed in Union uniforms stolen from Manassas Junction the previous week. One post-battle non-combatant letter also claimed that the rebels were falsely bearing the U.S. flag, in addition to Walcott's abovementioned "dark" uniforms.[69] These serious accusations are not considered plausible. When one considers that dusk was at hand, coupled with the natural darkness created by being in such thick woods, and that the Confederate gray or butternut uniforms would have naturally darkened when rain soaked, it is believed that the Union allegations were honest misrepresentations at best. When one also looks at the Victorian mindset of gallantry and honor that was so prevalent and personally important during these times, such intentional deceit is not feasible. In fact, in the latter years of the war, to be taken prisoner in the enemy's uniform was deemed by both sides as a hanging offense. Therefore, in consideration of the time of day, weather factors, and the soldiers' recollections, it is apparent that the 21st Massachusetts blindly stumbled into what amounted to an unplanned ambush, receiving what would be their worst loss of the war. Over two hundred men were killed or wounded in a brief moment of time, and the horrific psychological effect would linger with the survivors for weeks. One Massachusetts survivor wrote to his parents in the days to follow, "The boys are gradually getting over the battle of Chantilly. It was a scene I shall never forget. It was wholesale murder to stand at the muzzle of the enemy's guns and have a volley poured into us."[70]

The 51st Pennsylvania had been in line of march about one-half mile behind the 21st Massachusetts and was still posted to the rear of the action in support of Durell's battery which had now taken a position to the right and rear of the Reid house. Arriving with their horses on a full gallop, Kearny had placed the cannons at the edge of the cornfield. Their firing was hot, as the gunners quickly expended their ammunition throughout the battle. When they were down to almost the last round they started emptying the caisson from other cannons that had been disabled at the preceding Bull Run battle.[71] The supporting regiment, the 51st Pennsylvania, still remained in reserve and for reasons never made clear, was not involved in the thick of the fight. Nevertheless, their captain recalled that they certainly were close enough to feel and hear the thunder of Durell's cannon: "The grass in the field was very high, and in this we had to lay, right in rear of the battery, so close that blood ran out of our ears and noses, until one of the gunners told us to place a chip between our teeth and it would stop, and it had that result."[72]

Birney Arrives

West of the Ox Road, rain, casualties, low ammunition levels, and fatigue had taken their toll on Stevens' division. They had fallen back out of the woods and were barely holding their own within the grassy field. The arrival onto the scene of the 6th New Hampshire and 48th Pennsylvania from Colonel James Nagle's brigade added some reinforcements, and their addition to the left of the weakened 50th Pennsylvania at the southeastern edge of the cornfield stiffened the Pennsylvanians' resolve. It appeared to one New Hampshire officer arriving into the battle that the field had been deserted by every regiment except for the 50th Pennsylvania.[73] Another Granite Stater proudly recalled how one of his boys went right into it and fired 160 rounds during the fight. When the lad's musket became unusable from its excessive use he simply discarded it for a cleaner one from a wounded comrade.[74] Now the bluecoats faced another challenge, however. Poor visibility caused by the fast-approaching night as well as rain streaming off the men's kepis and into their eyes forced one man after another to aim in the general vicinity of the enemy instead of readily identifiable targets. "We fired at and for the flash of each others guns" wrote a diarist from the 48th. And as with all soldiers that night, the rain was having a disastrous effect on their gunpowder. "We fixed bayonets to repel any attempt of the rebels to charge upon us. And we stood our ground until Kearny came up." Kearny and his troops were now close at hand, with the general urging the New Hampshire men to "Hold out a little longer, boys, Kearny's division is coming to relieve you." Still, with the death of their divisional commanding officer, another assault against the rebel lines was out of the question. With reinforcements on the way, the 48th Pennsylvania held their ground on the hill just behind the Reid farm's apple orchard. Nearby, the 6th New Hampshire held their portion of the line by lying on the wet ground for the rest of the miserable night.[75] For those New Hampshire men, the cool, sodden night would be spent without oilcloths, blankets, or the contents of their knapsacks, all of which were hastily abandoned in the pell-mell retreat from Bull Run. Federal cavalry burned what they could after the fact to ensure the supplies not fall into Confederate hands.[76]

━━━━━━━━━━

Offensive maneuvers would have to be borne by others, and so it would be, for by that time General David Birney was arriving onto the scene with his huge 2nd Brigade from Kearny's 1st Division, III Corps. This brigade consisted of the 3rd and 4th Maine, the 1st, 38th, 40th, and 101st New York, along with the 57th Pennsylvania infantry regiments. Birney's seven-regiment brigade was larger than Stevens' entire division, which consisted of only six regiments. After briefly consulting with Reno and being appraised of the situation, Birney deployed his seven units along the southernmost edge of the cornfield and ordered them forward in battle line through the cornrows. The pressing need was to relieve Stevens' shattered division now located off to their right. With the sound of battle growing nearer, his regiments were sent forward at the double-quick. One New Yorker remembered that "We made ourselves as small as possible...as...the bullets began to play around our ears," with orders from their commanding colonel, John H. Ward, to "Look out for your ammunition, boys; keep your powder dry!"[77] The firefight was immediate and deadly, with the 4th Maine, who had advanced first on the far left of the Union line, taking a murderous barrage from Branch's North Carolinians at close range. Sensing they were being flanked, they fell back, claiming a "more advantageous position" on a small knoll where they poured hot lead into the woods and cornfield as fast as the weather would allow.[78] The 101st New York knelt in the field, aiming at the rebels at the edge of the woods. Men dropped quickly, one dismounted officer noting no doubt due to the clash of thunder and artillery, "the way the poor fellows fell was terrible, but not a groan or cry could you hear."[79] The 3rd Maine and 1st New York followed in quick succession, with Kearny using his trademarked short, spiriting phrases to urge them on. Kearny then rode toward the 40th New York "Mozart" regiment and announced, "Ah, my brave Forty boys! Always where I want you!" as he galloped to the head of the regiment. The 40th had been set under cover of the Reid farmhouse and its adjoining buildings with instructions to be ready for a charge in any direction. Kearny's final words to them stirred his men into action. "Now my gallant 40th, go in you have always driven the enemy and I know you always will."[80] A strong volley was received by the advancing New Yorkers who returned it "with interest," according to one private. "We fought for about three-quarters of an hour, the enemy 'peppering' us and we 'salting' them."[81] Only the 57th Pennsylvania was now left in line and members of Kearny's staff suggested that they also be sent to the advance, but Kearny had other plans for his Pennsylvanians. He told the staff to keep the Keystoners in reserve, then, nodding toward his advancing lines, Kearny remarked, "If these men have to retreat, I want them to fall back upon men that won't run!"[82] Kearny also brought up Captain George Randolph's Rhode Island battery to add firepower to the Yankee assault, but their ill-advised placement on a knoll directly in the rear of Birney's line rendered their effectiveness negligible. Being so close to the action, they were forced to use solid shot as opposed to exploding shells so as not to injure their own men. One hundred rounds later Randolph quieted his guns, unable to tell what effect he had had on the rebels.[83]

On the Confederate side, Branch's North Carolina Brigade had initially been placed in a position along the northwestern edge of the cornfield that allowed a flanking fire into Stevens' advance, but now Birney's advance had swung back to the left and was placing their own brigade in danger of being outflanked by the Federals. Branch moved the 18th North Carolina regiment from the center to the right, thereby quelling the threat but at a terrible cost to that regiment. Pender's 16th and 34th North Carolina Infantry had become separated from the rest of their brigade, but were in the thick of the fire with Branch's men and were suffering heavily from the flanking fire.[84] The brigade as a whole was now facing both low and wet ammunition problems and requested a withdrawal. When those facts were made clear to division commander A. P. Hill, he firmly ordered Branch to "hold his position at the point of the bayonet."[85] Such desperate measures may not have been necessary, for Hill still had Archer's

General Philip Kearny

and Lawton's brigades in reserve and both were within quick striking distance of the action, yet neither brigade was ever brought up. Why division commanders A. P. Hill and Alexander Lawton chose to keep these brigades well in reserve and out of all action is unknown to historians.

The bayonet was quickly becoming more operational than ornamental due to the number of muskets rendered useless by the downpour. Once into the cornfield, a Union bayonet charge was ordered which initially sent the rebels scurrying, but the outnumbered bluecoats were soon forced to back away.[86] The outgunned Federals soon realized that more reinforcements were desperately needed, so orders were quickly sent back to Colonel Orlando Poe, in command of Kearny's Third Brigade. His orders were to bring his men forward in support of the weakened left and to "fight the enemy wherever he finds them."[87] For the next hour and a half,

General Alexander R. Lawton
His debut as a divisional commander was inauspicious at best.

USAMHI

Kearny's brigade and their rebel foes jostled back and forth in the blood-stained cornfield, neither side gaining a lasting advantage. The entire panorama was later depicted by a Union combatant as a "desultory fight of regiments" that did not cease until their ammunition was either spent or unusable due to the rain. Several of the regiments, including the 3rd and 4th Maine, had virtually spent their entire allotment of cartridges and were holding their ground with the bayonet.[88] The weather, along with the coming night and the sloppy Virginia clay, brought about more personal clashes and hand-to-hand fighting within the cornfield and woods, a situation that was rare in the Civil War. Clubbed muskets and the bayonet had become weapons of choice.

About 6:00 P.M.—Phase 2: Birney's brigade advances
A "desultory fight of regiments"

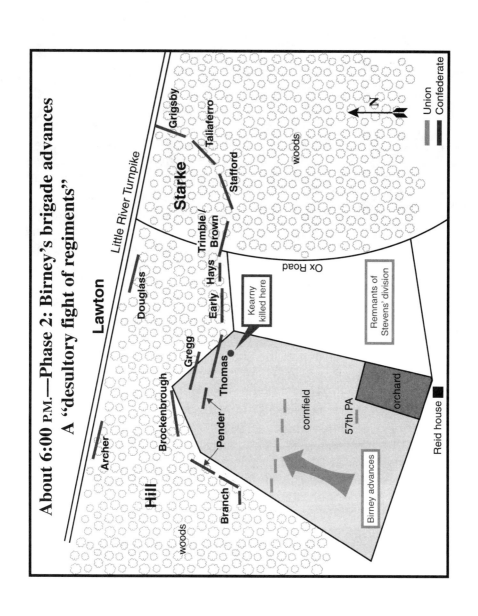

General David B. Birney

Massachusetts MOLLUS, USAMHI

With the battle raging in his front, Birney had become highly agitated over his perceived weakness and danger on his right flank. It appeared to him that Stevens' battered units had fallen back in disarray, therefore leaving his right flank open to attack from the east. The onset of darkness and the torrential rain allowed him no visibility to assess his dilemma. He quickly sent word to Kearny for support.

After receiving the call for assistance from Birney, Kearny pounded his horse to the action, disbelievingly stating to Birney upon his arrival that "Reno would not be such a fool as to leave the line open and not tell [you] of it!"[89] The thirty-seven-year-old Birney had been a brigade commander under Kearny for only a few months. He had been acquitted of the charge of disobeying an order at the battle of Seven Pines, yet Kearny's confidence in his subordinate's concerns was unshaken.[90] Kearny immediately dashed away and came across a few exhausted soldiers from the cut-up 79th New York standing on a ridge, where they had been regrouped by Captain William Lusk. The Highlanders had been slowly retiring soon after Stevens' death and their aborted charge into the woods.

Lusk later wrote that he found the color-bearer, the sixth in a twenty-minute span, "standing almost alone at the edge of some woods still clinging hopelessly to the colors." Kearny knew every man was desperately needed and promptly ordered his "Scotchmen" to follow him. When they advised him that they were all but out of ammunition, he replied, "Well, stand where you are and it may be that you will be able to assist me with the bayonet."[91]

The men of the 100th Pennsylvania "Roundhead" regiment were also slowly limping their way back and were attempting to reform their battered lines. Reverend Robert A. Brown, the regiment's chaplain, was with them when the general approached. He remembered that "General Kearny rode up and addressing me, inquired who we were and where was Col. (Lecky), and, when I had brought Col. L. to him, asked if we would support his battery just posted in an advanced position. The men answered with a cheer, and supported it amid the whistling balls till the enemy were driven off by the artillery and other divisions of infantry."[92] Racing forward, he then came across the battered 21st Massachusetts who had been cautiously making their way out of the Ox Hill woods east of the Ox Road and into the grassy field beyond. He frantically ordered them across the road exclaiming, "By God, they are cutting us off!"[93] They advised him of the uselessness of their weapons because of the driving rain, then pleaded for time to regroup and clean their muskets.[94] Kearny would have none of it, and was livid at their hesitation. He angrily urged the men forward, peppering the orders with "his sneers, threats and curses" while threatening the Bay Staters that he would order Randolph's battery to fire on them if they waited any longer. To add substance to his promise, Kearny galloped back to the Rhode Island gunners with orders to fire if the Massachusetts soldiers did not get moving.[95] Angered at Kearny's outburst, but not doubting the general's threat, the 21st began moving ahead, still tentatively, as it was now so dark that it was difficult to tell friend from foe. They had been joined by two of their companies who had managed to escape the ambuscade in the woods to the east and had now caught up to their comrades. Slowly they advanced in a northwesterly direction toward the cornfield. Their returning skirmishers, panting and out of breath, were adamant that the enemy was in force to their front. Kearny, who had been following close behind, did not believe it, claiming that the 21st was mistakenly firing on its own men. But when proof was shown to him in the guise of two rebel prisoners from the 49th Georgia just taken in their front, he cursed back at them, "God damn you and your prisoners!"[96] He wheeled his horse about and rode headlong into history.

Kearny's aide-de-camp, then-Lieutenant Charles Graves, recalled the scene: "We rode along the line, and General Kearny sent off one staff officer after another with orders, until I was the only one left with him. We finally arrived at the right of Stevens' line, where a battery was shelling the opposite woods. The General ordered me to ride at a gallop, back to General Pope, commanding one of our Brigades, and order him to 'double-quick' his brigade to that point and go into line. I did so, and returned as quickly as possible to the Battery. The rain was falling fast and darkness was coming on. I inquired of the Battery men which way General Kearny went, and they replied, pointing down to the right and front, 'that way.' 'My God,' was my exclamation, 'we have no troops there, he has ridden right into the enemy lines.'"[97] And so it proved. Artillerist Samuel Benjamin had been injured, and remembered lying on the ground within twenty feet of the general as he rode by, in the full light of the warming fire lit by his cannoneers. He called out to Kearny, frantically warning him that the Federal troops had been partially or even entirely withdrawn from the area, but the one-armed hero failed to respond.[98] Wanting to know for himself the nature of the ground and whether or not the woods were controlled by rebel troops, Kearny rode gallantly to his death. Union troops learned of the general's demise the next day from the Confederates who brought his body to them under a flag of truce. Apparently the general had unknowingly galloped up to a whole company of the enemy that had been positioned behind an old hedgerow. Since darkness had rendered their uniforms indistinguishable, Kearny called out, inquiring what units they were, and if there was room for him to form on their left. They immediately realized that a Union general was mounted in front of them at point-blank range. Rebel officers demanded that he surrender, but Kearny paid no heed. Attempting to shield himself with his horse's body, Kearny leaned over low on Bayard, wheeled the chestnut steed, and started back the way he came.[99] Shots rang out, at least one of which hit Kearny, killing him instantly.

Although many accounts have been written as to who killed the general and how he fell, it is accepted today that the fatal shot came from the 49th Georgia regiment of Thomas' brigade.[100] Was it also possible that orders were given not to fire on Kearny? One soldier in the 31st Virginia under Jubal Early, who would have had Kearny in his rifle sight just off to his right, strongly asserted in his memoirs that just such an order was given and that "if it was heard, it was disobeyed."[101]

In contrast to John Pope, Philip Kearny was one of those rare military men who inspired the utmost respect and admiration from both his men and the enemy. Unlike many Civil War generals, his modus operandi was at the fore, leading his men into battle, not well to the rear of the action. For this reason, men in his command idolized him. "Of all who have fallen in this war he is the only one for whom I have shed a tear. I have to confess that in spite of pride the news quite unmanned me," was a Michigan soldier's heartfelt sentiment

Death of General Kearny

shared by many a man in the Army of the Potomac.[102] Sergeant William Gardiner of the badly shot up 4th Maine offered a prayer for both the general and the army when he wrote to his sweetheart, "...peace to his ashes, and confusion to his enemies."[103] Nevertheless, Kearny's staunch reputation as a fearless and dashing commander was sometimes viewed by others as bordering on recklessness. Private James Stone of the 21st Massachusetts felt that Kearny was "entirely of his base that night. The way he ranted and swore around there was disgusting." Kearny's superior officer, General Samuel Heintzelman, recorded in his official report that Kearny "had rode forward alone to reconnoiter in his usual gallant, not to say reckless, manner, and came upon a rebel regiment."[104]

Kearny's body was removed from the field by the Confederates and taken to the vacant Chantilly mansion, which was about one and a half miles west of the modern-day Route 50/West Ox Road intersection.[105] Southern emotion toward the fallen warrior was equally honorable. Upon seeing the corpse of his old friend several hours later, Confederate General A. P. Hill sadly lamented, "Poor Kearny, he deserved a better death than this."[106] Papers that were on Kearny were rushed to Robert E. Lee in the event that they might hold some military significance, but a brief glance told the commanding general that they were of a "personal nature." Lee had them burned immediately out of respect for the Union general's privacy. Lee then dictated a brief letter to Union General Joseph Hooker offering to return Kearny's remains under a flag of truce. In the days to follow, Lee also saw to it that Kearny's horse, sword, and remaining personal accoutrements were returned to his widow.[107] The following morning, September 2, Stonewall Jackson rode by, saw the body and pointed out to the astonished rebels, "This is General Kearny." Not all were impressed, however. Edward McGinnis of the 1st Louisiana later recollected that "We were too busy with our meal and paid no attention....The fact is we saw so much of it that it was an everyday occurrence." When Jackson asked who had brought Kearny in, the reply was "those Georgians."[108]

Lieutenant George Beale of the 9th Virginia Cavalry sat in his saddle along the Little River Turnpike and watched Kearny's body pass by in an ambulance escorted by a detachment of infantry with their muskets reversed, a standard display of honor in martial funerals. Colonel Walter Taylor, Lee's chief aide, accompanied the general's remains and recognized that "there was no place for exultation in the contemplation of the death of so gallant a man....I was conscious of a feeling of deep respect and great admiration for the brave soldier, who, as stated by General Pope, had 'died as he would wish to die and as became his heroic character.'"[109] The Confederate procession marched several miles to the Union lines, where they were given a small meal in gratitude. The general's remains were received by five companies of the 57th Pennsylvania regiment, who then escorted his body into Alexandria for burial preparation.[110] According to Kearny's medical embalmers, he was killed by one bullet, which entered near the gluteus muscles close to the hip, ricocheted off the pelvic bone and ended in the center of the chest cavity.[111]

At the moment of Kearny's death, elements of Thomas' brigade had been advancing against Birney's right, but now surged against the front and flank of the 21st, ordering the Bay Staters to surrender. For the second time in less than an hour the 21st was caught completely off guard. The Confederate troops were so close that no man on either side had to aim; they simply lowered their guns and pulled the triggers. Captain Walcott recalled that "we gave what fire we could give them at a few paces distance, which they returned with interest."[112] Not one in ten rifles was serviceable owing to the weather, so those who had revolvers used them instead. Ammunition as well was soaked, and much of it unusable. According to Private Stone, "When the 'Johnnies' saw we were unable to return their fire, they appreciated the situation and over and through the fence they came to capture prisoners."[113] Men grappled and rolled in the mud in a death struggle as hand-to-hand fighting and bayonet thrusts were the state of affairs for about the next ten minutes. Walcott reminisced that as far as he knew, it was the first and last time that his Massachusetts comrades gave and received wounds with the bayonet. Men on both sides were physically exhausted from the effects of hand-to-hand fighting, and the continuing rain and lightning limited visibility to only a few yards in any direction. The darkness now rendered it impossible to tell friend from enemy, so by an unspoken but seemingly mutual agreement, both sides began slowly to withdraw, the fighting nearly over. The remnants of the 21st Massachusetts gathered around their mud-stained colors and fell back to the south.[114]

How crucial were the weather conditions to the proper usage of the Enfield rifle? This issue had been addressed almost six months earlier by Lieutenant William Clark of the 21st Massachusetts. In his report of the battle of New Berne, North Carolina, he noted, "Notwithstanding every precaution on the part of both officers and men very many of the rifles were rendered quite unserviceable by the moisture. In some the powder became too wet to ignite, and in very many of the Enfield rifled muskets the rammers were almost immovable from the swelling of the stocks. It is a great defect in this weapon that the friction of the wood along the whole length of the rammer is relied upon to keep it in place, since it is quite impossible that the rammers be well secured when the musket is dry and sufficiently loose for service when wet. It is a noteworthy evidence of discipline and courage on the part of the men that more than 50 went into the battle having only their bayonets to work with, and it was very hard to hear them in the thickest of the fight, while standing helpless in their places, beg their officers to give them a serviceable musket, and to see them eagerly seize the weapons of their comrades as fast as they fell beneath the leaden storm from the enemy's earthworks."[115] It is debatable whether even the most water-repellant muskets could have stood up to the deluge that night. Over a century later modern relic hunters have reported finding musket balls on the field with over sixty-five percent containing "extraction holes." Those corkscrew-like markings indicated that their owner was forced to remove them from the barrel in a fashion similar to removing a cork from a bottle. The frequency of misfirings due to wet powder is evidenced in the large numbers.[116]

—————

The audible cries of death's carnival were everywhere in the cornfield. Lieutenant George Parker of the 21st Massachusetts had fallen flat on his face the moment he heard the command of "fire" from the rebel colonel's lips. His quick reaction allowed his bowels and knees to stay where they were supposed to. With a lull in the fighting at hand, he slowly arose and began to assist and comfort his wounded comrades. The gargantuan task at hand simply overwhelmed him. "May I never hear such a cry as went up from that field....I had gone to every man and given them water or turned them over where they could die easier. As soon as they all knew I was with them—so many voices called me I knew not what to do—

'Oh for God's sake, Lt. Parker some water'—'oh don't leave me'...and even while I took away the canteen, his eyes would glaze and fix, for it was now bright moonlight and things could be seen plainly."[117] The lieutenant was granted permission by the Confederates to accompany his injured men who had been taken prisoner, among them the severely wounded captain of his regiment. They were escorted to a hospital behind the rebel lines where the captain's leg could be properly amputated.

He was also asked to come look at Philip Kearny's body to formally identify it. The general's coat and boots had already been confiscated, but Parker was assured by a Southern officer that they would be returned since "our boys didn't know who it was and thought it a nice thing to get hold of his clothes."[118]

Drenched clothes, exhaustion, and nightfall contributed to a desire of some front-line units to retire to the rear to regroup and catch their collective breaths since they believed the fight was over. Dr. Hunter Maguire, Stonewall's chief surgeon and apparently present at his side, recalled a legendary incident from Ox Hill regarding "Ol' Jack's" men leaving the field. "This faculty of knowing what they [his men] were doing was a great point with Jackson. I remember at Chantilly...that an aide-de-camp came up and said to General Jackson: 'General A. P. Hill asks permission to retire; his ammunition is wet.' 'Give my compliments to General Hill,' drawled Jackson, 'and tell him the Yankee ammunition is as wet as his—stay where he is.'"[119] It was an accepted fact in Stonewall's corps that the addressee was in store for a stern rebuke when Jackson began a reply with the phrase "Give my compliments to...."

On the Union side, Birney's now-exhausted brigade also began to pull slowly back from the cornfield, and in doing so it was noticed that "hardly a stalk was left standing in the whole field, except now and then a solitary one which had apparently escaped the storm of lead and was left a lonely sentinel to watch the remains of its companions."[120] There were not many men left standing in the field either. One New Yorker scribbled in his diary his simplistic, nightmarish memory of the carnage: "the rebels killed most all of us."[121] Lieutenant Theodore Dodge of the same regiment would have agreed, noting in his journal: "We went into this fight with over 250 men (many stragglers having come in). We were in some three quarters of an hour, and when the regiment came out, we had 5 officers and 30 men left."[122]

Colonel Orlando Poe's Third Brigade, consisting of the 2nd, 3rd, and 5th Michigan, 37th New York, and 99th Pennsylvania regiments, had now arrived on the scene behind Randolph's battery. The 5th Michigan was placed in support of the cannons while the rest of the brigade was instructed by Reno to hold, pending further orders. With darkness all around, and believing Kearny to be either dead or a prisoner, General David Birney assumed command of the division and sent Poe's brigade forward to relieve the 1st Brigade, which had exhausted practically all of its ammunition, as well as to aid whatever cohesive force was left of Stevens' battered regiments. Birney's 38th New York was replaced with the 2nd Michigan, the 40th New York with the 99th Pennsylvania, while the 3rd Michigan and 37th New York were placed in support.[123] Advancing through the pitch-black fields strewn with dead and wounded, the 2nd Michigan advanced within twenty rods of the rebel pickets and held their position. Along with the rain, a biting wind then came up from the northwest, causing many a drenched man to silently tremble in the cold of darkest night.[124]

With the battle winding down, the first regiments of Longstreet's division finally began arriving on the scene. The 1st Georgia regulars of General Tige Anderson's brigade were sent forward to assist if needed, as well as elements of Robert Toombs' brigade. One veteran remembered, "Anderson gave the order to fall in, take arms, double-quick, march and we were off down the road like a flash, leaving our baggage behind. We soon heard in front of us the booming of cannon and the rattle of musketry, and knew that the devil was to pay down the road

General James Longstreet

Miller, *Photographic History of the Civil War*

apiece."[125] "...As some of the boys expressed it, hell had broke loose again. We went over a mile, when we were halted in a lane and ordered by the right flank....In our front the Federals had several batteries of artillery and gave us what Teddy gave the drum. We certainly stuck might close to Mother Earth while the shells were trying to lop off the tree tops over our heads. We could not decide which was most to be feared, the shells or the limbs that came crashing down."[126]

Also arriving by wagon with Longstreet's men was the Confederate commanding general, Robert E. Lee. Still smarting from his fall and the resultant hand injuries of two days earlier, he had ventured far enough near the front lines to receive a worried warning from one of his aides. Standing in an open field with some staff near a farmhouse, Lee was told by the staffer returning from near the front that he was much too exposed standing where he was. When asked by Lee if he was sure, the aide replied, "Yes, sir,—it's hard to tell which comes fastest, rain drops or bullets." Lee was convinced to move away, but not at a speed to satisfy his worried aide-de-camp.[127]

Though relieving elements of Jackson's corps on the battlefield, Longstreet's wing was ultimately not engaged in the fight near Chantilly. Those units under Toombs and Anderson that had advanced into the woods were ultimately withdrawn to the road for bivouac.[128] Longstreet, known affectionately to his close friends as "Ol' Pete," was well aware that a sharp firefight had just occurred, based on his observation of the number of rebels streaming toward the rear in confusion. It was apparent that the victorious rout they had experienced two days earlier was not repeating itself. As he rode up to Jackson, he asked him about the situation at hand and then dryly remarked, "General, your men don't appear to work well today." "No," Jackson replied, "but I hope it will prove a victory in the morning."[129] For one of the few times in the Confederate chieftain's career, his expectations would be incorrect.

"The upturned faces of the dead" 5

Late Evening, September 1 to Early Morning, September 2

And so it was over. Darkness and fatigue, combined with water-damaged ammunition all conspired to bring about an unspoken, but mutual end to the fighting. For all of the helter-skelter fighting within the cornfield, the neighboring grassy field, and the surrounding woods, neither side had gained any ground from when the battle began. A Union cavalryman surveying the ground poetically wrote: "...and as the thunder of heaven died away in the murmuring distance, and the pure drops of rain ceased to baptize anew the surface of the bloodstained earth, the rebel force drew back from the encounter."[1]

Both sides posted their pickets between the respective lines as a form of early warning system, but the night was so black that no man could see more than three feet in front of him. Longstreet's fresh troops stumbled to their positions with each man's hand on the cartridge box of the man in front of him, so as to not get lost in the pitch blackness. The front lines were so close that the rebel pickets could hear distinctly the conversations of their enemy, while rebel campfires were clearly visible to Federal soldiers just beyond the woods.[2] Nobody dared move, nor wanted to; nevertheless a few unfortunates on each side accidentally wandered into the other line only to discover rudely that they were now prisoners of war. One careless rebel adjutant strolled unassumingly into a picket post belonging to the 51st Pennsylvania. When he replied to their question as to what regiment he belonged with a nonchalant, "3rd Louisiana,"

Private John Seibert happily exclaimed, "then by damn, you're my prisoner for mine is the 51st Pennsylvania!"[3] Night slowly progressed and by 9:00 P.M. only the occasional shot rang out between the pickets of both sides, yet a large skirmish of a different sort was building within Union headquarters. With the battle over, a lieutenant colonel of the 79th New York sent word back to corps commander Jesse Reno that the rebels had been driven back, but that General Isaac Stevens had fallen in battle. Reno hastily responded with orders to bury Stevens on the field, and then to fall back, to the total indignation of the men of the 79th. They simply refused to bury their beloved general in the mud of an unknown field. His body was placed in an ambulance and sent to the Reid house, now in use as a Union field hospital, from which his remains were later sent back to Washington.[4] Once there, John Hayes, an old friend of Stevens', took charge of his funeral. At the family's request, the ceremony took place in Newport, Rhode Island, and attracted politicians and friends from all over the northeast. Eulogies flowed in from as far away as the Pacific Northwest and typical was the beginning of a long poem that appeared in a Boston paper:

> He fell—that glowing eye
> In sudden night was quenched;
> But still the flag he lifted high
> And onward bore to victory,
> In his dead hand was clenched.

Stevens was posthumously promoted to the rank of major general, retroactive to July 4, 1862. Such was the regard for Stevens in Washington that rumors circulated at the time of his death said that Lincoln was considering Isaac Stevens for command of the Army of Virginia.[5] In his moment of shining glory at Ox Hill, Stevens displayed the characteristics that had prompted such consideration: courage, decisive action, organizational skills, and a superb knowledge of tactics. The last of these was most evident in his Jackson-like strike at the flank of the enemy. Though potentially outnumbered three to one, Stevens' concerted charge against the center of the Confederate line put the enemy on their heels from the beginning of the fight, a situation from which they never fully recovered. Simply put, Isaac Stevens' daring arguably saved Washington and John Pope's Union army.

As is no doubt the case in any hard fight, the men were able to pause and reflect on how it was that they were still alive, when so many friends and comrades around them had fallen. Two weeks later, William Behan of the 5th Louisiana wrote home stating that a bullet had splintered his rifle stock while he was in the process of aiming, four minié balls had shredded his clothing, and most of his trousers had been blown off by an exploding shell, yet he had somehow emerged unscathed from Chantilly.[6]

Attention was now turned to personal needs such as food, a warm beverage, and getting dry. Confederate stomachs were especially empty, and as most of their haversacks were bare, they focused on Union dead or wounded. The following rebel reminiscence from Ox Hill was no doubt typical of many men and battlefields: "That night, when all was still and darkness had settled upon the field where lay the victims of war, a soldier of the 40th regiment, an intrepid Irishman, George Cromwell by name, went out prowling for food and plunder, taking his musket with him. Unexpectedly, meeting a Federal lieutenant and four men bearing a stretcher and searching for their wounded captain, he was asked to what regiment he belonged. With ready wit he named a New York regiment, and then learning their business and finding that they were unarmed, he leveled his musket, demanded their surrender, and brought them as prisoners within our lines. I myself did a little searching until I found a full haversack strapped to a man who would never use his teeth again. I was hungry, and chilled by the recent rain. I found in the haversack crackers and ground coffee mixed with sugar; and bringing into requisition my matches, tin cup, and canteen of water (which three things I was always careful to have about me), I soon had a pint of steaming beverage. I ate my supper, and then laid down to sleep. This was only one of many times that I slept in wet garments on the rain-soaked lap of earth without injury to my health; and the only reason I can give for the immunity is, that those were war times."[7]

With the enemy so near, many drenched, front-line Confederates were forced to sleep that night on the soggy, cold earth without benefit of fires, lest their position be given away to the opposition.[8] Longstreet's newly arriving men were dispersed that night to form a line slightly to the rear of where Jackson's men had fallen back to, believing that they were about fifty yards behind their pickets. They held that position on wet ground throughout the night. The rear elements under Longstreet were still as far back as Pleasant Valley and had a more agreeable night as they slept on a bed of dry straw. Private Benjamin Farinholt of the 53rd Virginia wrote in his diary that "We bivouacked in a large oak grove...we took down six large stacks of hay. Each man an armful to make a bed of...I never saw larger stacks of hay and certainly never saw any disappear so quickly."[9] Meanwhile, Jackson's battered brigades were relieved to a fresh line behind Longstreet's new arrivals to regroup, to the unpleasant surprise of some of Longstreet's men when they awoke next morning. "Imagine our astonishment, as the tedious, dragging night at last gave way to the coming morning, to find ourselves *facing our line* and between it and the enemy! Front to rear was soon ordered...."[10]

The same orders regarding no fires were also given to the front line Union soldiers. For many a soldier, that night of September 1 presented the most brutal weather they had endured in the war. Many Federals lost their knapsacks and blankets in the retreat from Bull Run and were forced to spend the cool black night with no cover at all. A few unfortunates even had no shirt. Exhaustion claimed many as they collapsed to the ground, weary, wet, and hungry as they went to sleep, impervious to the chilling rain that continued to fall.[11] Captain Thomas Parker of the 51st Pennsylvania later recalled that "Their condition [could] safely be compared to that of a man being compelled to stand in cold water up to his chin for eight hours in succession."[12] Luck was with many men farther back from the front however, as they were able to kindle large fires to dry their saturated clothing. Orders were given around 2:00 A.M. of the 2nd to renew the fires, to give the rebels the impression that they intended on staying in position for the remainder of the night. Sleep was not forthcoming, however, for one-half hour later the order to march was given and the exhausted and wet Northern men set out for the Warrenton Pike.[13]

Since the conclusion of the battle, the Union side of the field had been guarded by the relatively fresh troops from Poe's Third Brigade and Robinson's First Brigade, with the latter having moved into the grassy ground off to Birney's right. Here they were buttressed

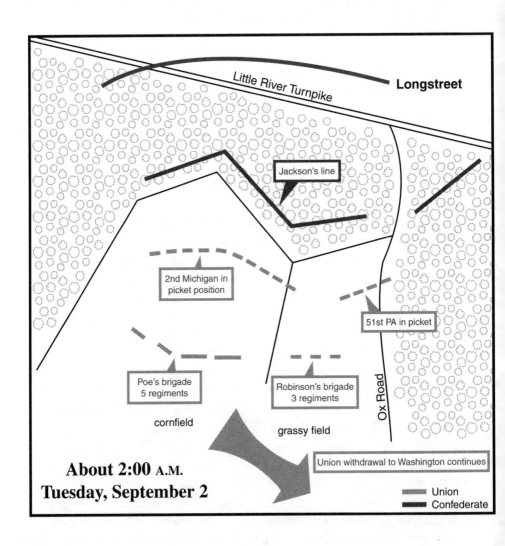

Little River Turnpike

Longstreet

Jackson's line

2nd Michigan in picket position

51st PA in picket

Poe's brigade 5 regiments

Robinson's brigade 3 regiments

cornfield

grassy field

Ox Road

Union withdrawal to Washington continues

About 2:00 A.M.
Tuesday, September 2

Union
Confederate

General Orlando M. Poe

He was then colonel of the 2nd Michigan Infantry at Ox Hill and commanded Kearny's Third Brigade, which held the field after the firing subsided.

by the previously uninvolved 51st Pennsylvania, which throughout the fight had acted only as support for Durell's artillery, but was now picketing across the grass field and Ox Road. Ultimately, neither Poe's nor Robinson's brigade fired shots in anger, but successfully held the field for the retreating Federals. Hungry, wet, and weary, Poe's and Robinson's men also began the slow withdrawal back to Fairfax Court House, following Birney's Second Brigade. Only the 2nd Michigan was left behind as pickets, and then as rear guard to cover the Federal retreat. Robinson's brigade, like all the others, was longing just to make it back into

General John Robinson
Miller, *Photographic History of the Civil War*

the safety of the capital. A few days later, they would be bivouacked on Arlington Heights, the site of Robert E. Lee's pre-war home. There, they would begin the road to emotional and physical recovery.[14]

For the second night of the past three, a continuous line of worn-out men in blue, with horses and wagons, filled the Warrenton Pike as they rumbled eastward toward the safety of Washington. With the artillery of man and nature having ceased, there was "nothing to be heard but the dry, hoarse cough from those soldiers who have caught a severe cold from the effects of the late storm, which may be the cause of some poor fellows death, offered up for the good cause."[15] The same miserable conditions affected the Federal defensive lines at Germantown. Lying in their rifle pits, with their boots filled with water, the average private had no idea whether an attack was forthcoming. Thoughts turned to warm sunlight and hot coffee. One Johnny Yank remembered, "We were wet through and the ground was soaking, so that there was nothing else to do except to wander about disconsolately waiting for the day to come."[16]

Accordingly, the Ox Field battlefield that cold and wet night would belong to the Confederates—and the lifeless bodies of the heroes. One solitary survivor of the 6th Louisiana recalled how they provided him the only company. "We camped on the field, sleeping side by side with the dead of both armies. It was very dark; occasionally the moon would come from under a cloud and show the upturned faces of the dead, eyes wide open seeming to look you in the face."[17]

"A beastly, comfortless conflict"   6

Medical and Casualty Situation in the Aftermath

The fight at Ox Hill raged for only about three hours, yet some regiments engaged there suffered higher losses than in the entire three days at Second Manassas. In that battle no field general had been killed, but two of the Union army's most promising and respected commanders fell in the brief engagement near Chantilly. Federal losses of dead, wounded, and captured totaled approximately one thousand while Confederate casualties were in the five to six hundred range. Actual troop casualties at Ox Hill are difficult to determine as some units included their losses with those incurred at Manassas, so, at best, historians have been left over the years with educated guesses. What can clearly be ascertained, though, is that at the height of the battle, Stonewall Jackson had his entire corps— fourteen infantry brigades strong totaling some fifteen thousand men—arrayed in line of battle against seven Union brigades commanding no more than six thousand men. Yet until darkness swept over the field, the outcome was in doubt, and for brief moments during Stevens' charge, victory was within Federal reach. As a percentage of troops engaged, Union losses were substantially higher than those of the Confederates. Considering the short amount of time that the battle actually raged, Chantilly was indeed a "beastly, comfortless conflict."[1]

All battles were inevitably bloody affairs with scores of wounded and dying men strewn throughout the battle area both during and after the battle. Chantilly was no exception, as surgeons on both sides commenced their grisly work of sawing off limbs and making their troops as comfortable as possible. The flow of men into the various fields and houses that had been converted into hospitals quickly overwhelmed the surgeons, who, as in all battles, had to prioritize their work.[2] Many of the blue-clad wounded with relatively minor injuries, and who could still walk, were told by the harried Union surgeons to continue on their own toward Fairfax.[3]

An Alabamian belonging to Trimble's brigade whose head had been on the receiving end of Yankee shrapnel managed to stagger to the field hospital, but as he had no shattered limbs, would not immediately be seen by the doctors. "I felt the blood trickling down my face but was hardly conscious of my condition. I do not remember how I made my way....Someone felt my head and told me I was badly hurt. Several pieces of the outer skull bone came out and I began to suffer great pain....I do not know how I did it but I filled my canteen with water, punched a hole at the bottom and hung it up on a nail in the wall. I then lay down on the floor and let the water slowly drip on the wound. I kept this up all night and the next morning felt somewhat relieved but was in a semi-dazed condition."[4] The surgeon of the 20th South Carolina (Dr. Spencer Welch) reported, "...I went into a horse lot and established a field infirmary, and saw an old lady and her daughter fleeing from a cottage and crossing the lot in the rain. The old lady could not keep up and the daughter kept stopping and urging her mother to hurry. The bullets were striking all about the yard of their house. Lt. Leopard from Lexington was brought back to me with both his legs blown off below the knees by a shell, and another man with part of his arm torn off, but neither Dr. Kennedy, Dr. Kilgore, nor our medical wagon was with us, and I had nothing with me to give them but morphine. Both men died during the night....We filled the carriage house, barn and stable with our wounded, but I could do but little for them....After doing all I could for the wounded, my brother, my servant Wilson, and myself went into the orchard and took pine poles from a fence and spread them on the wet ground to sleep on. I discovered a small chicken roosting in a peach tree and caught it, and Wilson skinned it and broiled it, and it was all we three had to eat that day. Wilson got two good blankets off the battlefield with U.S. on them, and we spread one on the poles and covered with the other."[5]

Northern soldiers were no better off, and inevitably had higher casualties as they had taken the initiative throughout much of the battle.

Darkness added to the confusion that seemed to reign after the battle. A soldier in the 5th New Jersey recalled, "In the woods close to our line was a large fire, toward which all the wounded who could walk came expecting to find the surgeon and get their wounds dressed. No surgeon was there, and no one knew where to find them. One man came along while I was standing there to warm myself who was shot in the head, and the blood was still running down his face. Finding no one there to attend to him, he traveled off in the rain."[6]

Making men comfortable often consisted of a shot of whiskey or, if lucky, a dash of chloroform. These simple painkillers were not always present, especially when impromptu "hospitals" were set up. Many a grisly scene existed. "(I) saw some surgeons operating on some wounded men who were to be sent on to Alexandria by train. One of them had his leg cut off above the knee, and when we arrived the surgeon was tying up the arteries. The stump looked like a piece of raw beef. The other man had a part of his foot taken off. Neither off them seemed to be under the influence of chloroform, but were held down by some four men, while nothing but a groan escaped them, as the operation proceeded."[7]

Word of scores of men wounded during the carnage at Second Bull Run prompted one of the earliest excursions of Clara Barton onto a Civil War battlefield. Later known as the "Angel of the Battlefield," and the future founder of the American Red Cross, Barton had made her first approved foray onto a battlefield almost a month before at the battle of Cedar Mountain. The Massachusetts native was then a resident of Washington, D.C., and the rumored bloodbath was proving too much for her to ignore. For months, Barton had asked for medical supply donations from family and friends back in her home state. Items such as bandages, blankets, and dry food items were in constant need. She spent her time between the battles of Cedar Mountain and Second Manassas in Washington tending to the wounded at local hospitals, paying especially close attention to her fellow Bay Staters. Barton's diary records that on August 30 Barton visited Sergeant Field of the 21st Massachusetts at the Armory Hospital and took him a comb.[8] Shortly thereafter she and several friends managed to get their stores onto a train headed to Fairfax Station. Working with Dr. James Dunn, she and her assistants administered

Modern view of St. Mary's Church

On its slopes, Clara Barton cared for Union casualties from Ox Hill and Manassas. Her character as the "Angel of the Battlefield" was born.

Collection of the author

care to over three thousand wounded soldiers, who were gently placed on straw in the middle of a field and on the gentle slopes of St. Mary's Church surrounding Fairfax Station. Working with two lanterns and candles, it was next to impossible to move about in the dark as the wounded men were laid so close together. Barton recognized a few of the men belonging to the 21st Massachusetts. Like her, the regiment had hailed from Worcester County, and several of the men had been her students in her prior life as an educator. When they relayed the horror that had befallen them on the slopes of Ox Hill, she was aghast, but nevertheless felt an abiding fervor at their bravery. Her pride was evident when she wrote to her friend Lizzie Shaver several days later: "The old 21st Mass. lay between us and the enemy and they couldn't pass....And the courage of the man who braved death in the darkness at Chantilly let no man question."[9] The supplies she brought with her went quickly, and in the end, Clara was offering up the meat from her own sandwiches. When the food disappeared she gathered up army hardtack[10] from the knapsacks of the wounded, pulverized the crackers into small crumbs, and then blended them with a sweet concoction of whiskey, wine, water, and brown sugar. This blend she spoon-fed to the injured as they were loaded into the waiting freight cars which would take them to hospitals in Alexandria. To her credit, she stayed to the last, and on the morning and afternoon of September 2 helped to oversee the evacuation of the wounded. By 3:00 P.M. Rebel cavalry had been spotted in the surrounding hills. A worried Union officer asked her if she could escape on a bareback horse if need be. Barton answered in the affirmative, thereby buying herself a few more precious minutes to minister. When a rebel sniper opened fire on them from the nearby woods, it became obvious it was time to leave.[11]

After frantically making sure that all the wounded were on board, she stood on the end of the last train as it pulled away. The last orders from General Herman Haupt, stationed in Alexandria, and in charge of the Union railroad system, was that the station and its related stores be destroyed in case of attack by Confederate cavalry. The final wire from the station to Haupt was soon sent by the dispatcher, a man known only by the name of McCrickett. His final transcription were the words, "Have fired it. Goodbye."[12] By 5:00 P.M. Fairfax Station and her makeshift hospital were aflame. Barton's final glance back at the place where she had offered food and medicine to the dying revealed Confederate cavalry swooping in to the station. Nevertheless, the Union's rush to evacuate had been so great that rebel troopers were able to salvage ample quantities of badly needed supplies from the inferno.[13]

Fifty years later, survivors of the 21st Massachusetts, which had been butchered in the woods of Ox Hill, still remembered Barton's tender mercies. Veteran Charles Simmons wrote: "The survivors of the Veteran 21st Massachusetts Regiment...wish to put on record, the day of your coming to us at Bull Run and Chantilly, when we were in our deepest bereavement and loss; how your presence and deeds brought assurance and comfort...."[14]

Retreat to Washington

It was certainly a scene of chaos on the Warrenton Pike as Union soldiers and teamsters attempted to navigate the narrow dirt road. "Several wagon trains became jammed together on the turnpike and a great panic ensued. Wagons were two or three abreast, and the mules going at a full gallop. There came a sudden crash and a jam, and wild cursing and shouting by the drivers."[15] The road was simply too clogged with battle-weary soldiers to allow a normal march. "Sometimes we marched about ten or fifteen steps, and then halted. We got so tired out through this, besides it being in the night and in big woods, that when the word came 'Halt!' we dropped down, and when we were down came the words, 'Forward March!' The dropping down and getting up, perhaps two hundred times, or much oftener, was tiresome beyond description."[16] Numerous injuries occurred to both man and beast fleeing eastward on the Warrenton Pike.

The chaotic rush to exit back to the safety of Washington caused for some an even greater horror than a quick death on the field of battle; that being a slow death from wounds and starvation. "It is the one thing a soldier dreads most, thus to be left wounded on the battle field, to linger perhaps for days, and then to die, with the pangs of hunger and thirst added to those of his neglected wounds."[17] Unfortunately, this dreaded fate was to be realized for many, as scores of Union wounded were left behind at Manassas and Chantilly during the withdrawal of the army. Dr. Calvin Cutter, surgeon of the 21st Massachusetts, bemoaned that fact in his diary the day after Ox Hill, recording: "Some three hundred wounded. No aid sent to them. No men to give them water,"[18] while a Union diarist in Washington wrote on September 3 that "Dr. Johnson of the Michigan cavalry just called in and tells me he is from the late battlefield...He says he leaves on the field between two and three thousand of our wounded who are perishing with hunger."[19] Confederate soldiers offered some help, but had their hands full caring for their own. By the morning of September 3, the Confederates were also leaving the battlefield. A handful of Union soldiers who were left behind did what they could, but the task was daunting. Virtually no food was available, and what little there was had to be found by the wounded crawling from one haversack to another.

The Virginia heat was intense in the days following Ox Hill and Manassas, and only added to the woes of those left behind. The carnage drew hordes of flies and their resultant natural horrors, all the while moans of "water, water" hummed across the blood-stained field.[20]

This sorry state of affairs was well known to those in Union authority. A circular pinned to the Federal Treasury building let all know that scores of Union casualties were left unattended on the Manassas battlefield. This prompted Secretary of War Edwin Stanton to issue an appeal through the Washington papers asking doctors and male nurses to ride out to the Manassas battlefield to assist with the wounded. Medicinal stimulants, as well as brandy and whiskey were brought along, allegedly to ease the suffering of the wounded. Unfortunately, these supplies were discovered by many of the "nurses," who ended up drinking the spirits to ease the monotony of the all-night train trip. The results were predictable and disastrous. Scores of civilians arrived drunk and disorderly, to the total dismay of Union officers. Haupt was livid, ordering the drunken rabble back to Washington with requests to the Assistant Secretary of War P. H. Watson that no more be allowed to come out. They were promptly put on the next train back to Alexandria, leaving legitimate doctors in that town under the impression that no additional help was needed.[21]

Federal commanders now faced not only the knowledge of the grievous condition of their comrades but the embarrassment of having to again ask the enemy for permission under a flag of truce to retrieve their men. In a letter to Lee on the third, General Jesse Reno wrote: "Sir: I have just received information through Chaplain Ball, of Twenty-first Massachusetts Volunteers, that about 250 of our wounded are now lying upon the battle-field of 1st instant entirely destitute of medical attendance and provisions. I therefore respectfully request your permission to send forward, under flag of truce, Chaplain Ball and the medical director of this command, with the necessary medical stores and provisions for the comfort of these wounded, and to bring away such of them as are able to be removed."[22] Intentions and results apparently did not mesh all that well, for almost a week later on September 9, Surgeon General William Hammond tersely reported to Secretary of War Edwin Stanton that "...Up to this date 600 wounded still remain on the battle-field in consequence of an insufficiency of ambulances and the want of a proper system for regulating their removal in the Army of Virginia. Many have died of starvation; many more will die in consequence of exhaustion, and all have endured torments which might have been avoided." Others pinned the blame for the lack of ambulances and medical stores not with the army medical corps, but rather on the rebels themselves, claiming that forty-two fully laden medical wagons had been captured by the Confederates at Manassas Junction the week before.[23] Understanding that capturing the enemy's stores is a fundamental goal in war apparently escaped their attention.

The consequences of inadequate care for the wounded revisited the Union soldiers stationed in Fairfax County during the coming winter. Less than four months after the Chantilly battle, members of various Vermont regiments were stationed near Fairfax Court House during the holiday season of 1862. They visited the battlefield over the holidays so that they could see the spots where Generals Stevens and Kearny had fallen, and to pay their final respects. The grotesque human remains from the horrific three-hour battle were still evident. The men observed that their comrades from the 12th Vermont were burying numerous corpses, and in some needy cases, reburying the fallen. It was certainly difficult to determine which side, if either, had obtained the better burial. One Vermonter noted that the Confederates, who had been left in control of the field, seemed to have been able to bury their dead in proper graves, but many Union soldiers had only a few shovel-fulls of dirt tossed over them. It was noted that in many cases legs, feet and arms were exposed, with the flesh still on.[24] On the other hand, Private William Knight wrote of the scene to his wife, noting: "the road all along [Fairfax] we found strewn with broken muskets knapsacks &c. We crossed the battlefield of chantilla [sic], the men on our side appeared to be buried well but those that appeared to be on the rebel side were scersely [sic] covered up. I saw one that was thrown into a ditch head to the south, his head was above the surface of the earth. this looks rather hard to a green Vermonter I tell you."[25]

The ravages of war also brought about another type of casualty to Fairfax County: the displacement and uprooting of the civilian population. The Charles Calvin Stuart family of Chantilly had by no means been alone in their fleeing the close proximity of battle. The northern Virginia countryside had been ravaged by the war, in most places presenting a barren, lunarlike landscape. Colonel John Magruder, commander of the 57th Virginia, observed on the Confederate march that "The whole section of country from Haymarket to this point is a perfect wilderness, without a single inhabitant as far as I am aware—it's a distance of perhaps twelve miles—the land is mostly poor—deserted dwellings numerous."[26] Trees and fences were gone, used by both armies for firewood; fields of vegetables and corn had been foraged clean; livestock slaughtered and wells drained to feed and quench the thirst of marching armies. Due to the constant encampment by one army or the other for over a year, Centreville had become "a dilapidated village" with no more than thirty private houses, all confiscated for army hospital use. Gardens were destroyed and other homes had been completely gutted or even torn down to furnish gun platforms in the old rebel fort.[27] This annihilation of the land was not limited to the immediate battlefield area, but had spread to all of northern Virginia. Wrote Private Knight of the 16th Vermont: "From here to fairfax Court I saw nothing worthy of note only the roads were lined with dead horses & mules & what we see everywhere here deserted plantations & mutilated buildings for when the union soldiers come to an old secesh, rip goes his shanty."[28] The courthouse at Fairfax had long ceased serving any legal function by the time the Ox Hill battle was over, and was now strictly a Union military headquarters, gutted of all papers and furniture. The little village, which had at one point housed three hundred residents, was transformed into a military camp, presenting an anthill-like quality as soldiers scurried about.

Unwilling to put up with any more, families who had resided near the Manassas and Ox Hill battlefields were fleeing. Many women, children, and contrabands joined the retreating Union army eastward into Alexandria.[29] One local, Maria Barlow, wrote later in December 1862 that "Fairfax will be depopulated. Barnett King starts for Ohio tomorrow morning with all his family....Mrs. Cockerille it is rumored will leave....Mr. Machen's folks have gone to Baltimore." Pondering her own decision to stay, along with the fate of the plundered Chantilly mansion, Barlow wrote: "It is not for present enjoyment that anyone stays; it is for the protection of home only—hoping at some future day it may be enjoyed. To see the fate of vacated buildings in the last visit of the army is to see total destruction."[30] If not literally precise, Maria Barlow's prediction had a ring of accuracy as a haunting depiction from the end of the war observed, "From Alexandria to the [Manassas] battlefield is one wide area of desolation. Fences are utterly swept away. Here and there a dilapidated house shelters a few squalid inmates, and occasionally a small patch of corn or wheat is passed, but the whole face of the country is changed. Scrub oak and pine are springing up everywhere."[31]

Afterward and the Days to Follow

Synopsis

The battle of Ox Hill was one of a few engagements during the war that ended without a clear-cut victor, thereby enabling proponents of both sides to forever claim that their forces triumphed. Since Pope's Northern forces suffered more casualties and abandoned the field first, Confederates could claim victory under the old military tradition that he who leaves the field first has lost. Nevertheless, it is the opinion of the author that the Chantilly-area battle, when viewed within its own context, was a somewhat hollow tactical Union victory. To be sure, the entire campaign up to that point had been a smashing Confederate triumph, but Lee's new, primary goal after August 30 was to pursue and destroy Pope's weakened army, and then perhaps place Washington in his sights. Though he had soundly whipped Pope at Second Manassas, the Federal army was still cohesive, dangerous, and able to fight. By the morning of September 2, most of Pope's army was secure on their retreat to the capital. Lee's goal of destroying the Union Army of Virginia was not achieved.

The frantic aim of Union generals after Second Manassas was simply to secure the safety of the army, and likewise that of Washington. This was initially accomplished by retreating behind the strong Union fortifications at Centreville, thereby placing the army between Lee and Washington, and finally confirmed when it became apparent that a rebel strike at Washington was not forthcoming.

By extension, what saved Washington was not the main battle near Chantilly, but rather Pope's heavy reinforcing of his men at

Germantown that helped cause Jackson to delay his march of attack, half-hearted as it was. This delay allowed Stevens time to bring
up his division and surprise Jackson, in consequence forcing the
battle to be fought in the first place. Had that consistent reinforcing
throughout the 31st and the 1st not occurred, it can be surmised
that Jackson may have succeeded in getting behind Pope, and then
destroying the Federal army in detail. This hypothetical scenario was
not lost on Union participants either. Lieutenant Horatio Belcher of
the 8th Michigan understood the magnitude of what had just transpired when he acknowledged in his diary, "Had we been defeated
again here our army would have been annihilated and Washington
taken."[1] The Union army's last-minute success at Ox Hill is what
ultimately prompted quite a few Union participants to proclaim
Chantilly their victory, albeit a small one, under the guise that the
planned Confederate strike on Washington had been repulsed.

Though numerous rebel
foot soldiers wrote in their diaries
and letters that they had whipped
the Yanks once again, opposition
to the Union claim of victory from
Confederate generals or colonels
was conspicuously absent. The
day after the battle, Southern
general William Dorsey Pender,
whose Tar Heel brigade was in
the thick of it, wrote to his wife
regarding the fight: "The Yankees
had rather the best of it as they
maintained their ground and accomplished the object which was
to cover their retreat...none of us
seemed anxious or did ourselves
much credit." The general also
gruffly complained with his pen
that he had lost the equivalent of

**General
William Dorsey Pender**

Confederate Military History, Vol. 5

two regiments during the battle due solely to straggling.[2] Realizing
that they had accomplished nothing at Ox Hill, E. Porter Alexander,
Lee's uninvolved chief artillerist, later recollected, "It was, under the
circumstances, a useless affair. There was little chance of either

side accomplishing any result beyond the killing of a few opponents with probably equal results to itself."[3] A very accurate sentiment, as the battle of Ox Hill played no role in the final tactical outcome of the just-concluded campaign, save for the deaths of two of the Union army's finest field generals.

The Battle of Flint Hill

The bleary-eyed Confederates who were allowed to doze awoke on the 2nd concerned that their front lines were still very near the enemy. The cold, wet ground had ensured a miserable night's sleep. Private Alexander Hunter never forgot that "We awoke so stiff and rigid that it took us some time to straighten our limbs. Our bodies were chilled through, but to our great delight the sun's warm beams darted through the rift in the clouds, and dried the wet clothes, but still our condition was deplorable."[4] Unsure of Federal intent, many men were ordered to lie still in their front lines throughout most of the day. Many of the wagons had yet to arrive with rations, so Confederate stomachs had to make do with a breakfast consisting of chewing the substance from sassafras twigs. By noon, a few wagons were finally arriving, including one laden with bread, hams, cakes and other delicacies sent by the Confederate ladies of Leesburg. Still fearful of a Yankee attack, a few men would be sent back to cook up rations and then bring them forward to the men in the front line.[5]

On the Union side, the entire army of Virginia, with the exception of Hooker's command at Germantown, was now in full flight back to the safety of Washington's entrenchments. Any thought of renewing the attack was off the table. Many of the men who had not participated in the previous night's melee at Ox Hill were now hearing word of its ferocity, and learning for the first time of Stevens' and Kearny's deaths. But to the typical private, the immediate issues were the same as his Confederate counterpart's, food and rest. At Fairfax Court House, Private Alfred Bellard recalled that his 5th New Jersey regiment gathered up all the fence rails they could find for firewood to make their morning coffee. They then went to work on a nearby farmhouse when the fence rails gave out, only relenting when an officer ordered them to cease their destruction. Their retreat eastward began again shortly after noon, during which lunch was offered up when wagons filled with fresh loaves of bread arrived from the ladies of Alexandria. "As we marched past every man was handed a loaf."[6]

The only shots fired on September 2 were delivered by Union General Edwin Sumner's rear guard and Jeb Stuart's rebel cavalry, who continued to harass the flanks of the retreating Federal column in the vicinity of Fairfax Court House. The Northern men were covered in dirt and mud from the previous day's weather, plus a film of bitter defeat was blanketing them as well. The continuous rain had turned the roads into a quagmire of muck so thick that in some places it swallowed a man's foot up beyond the ankle and took his shoe right off his foot. Strict orders were given that there was to be no stopping for lost shoes.[7]

Earlier that morning, Confederate cavalry General Wade Hampton had arrived on the scene with his mounted brigade from Charles City, (West) Virginia. The sight of scores of exhausted and wounded rebel infantry correctly convinced one diarist from Hampton's brigade that "we got a little the worst of it" the previous day at Ox Hill.[8] Stuart wanted to waste no time in pressing the attack and promptly sent Hampton's troopers with several pieces of horse artillery to the vicinity of Flint Hill to try to once again flank the fast retreating bluecoats. The pounding horsemen had not far to ride before they started rounding up Yankee stragglers. Rebel Private Samuel Elias recalled how they were told that the Union main body was always "just ahead of you, boys."[9] Hampton had developed the trait of personally scouting out his planned operations and this morning offered a near tragic portent of what would later befall other senior Confederate generals. Thinking him a Federal soldier, a lone rider from his 1st North Carolina Cavalry had the large-built general in his musket sight, only lowering his rifle at the last possible instant when he recognized the palmetto state seal on the South Carolinian's broad hat. "But it's no joke, he came as near as a gnat's heel of ketchin' it that time," remarked the Tarheel horseman. "Lord, I would a hated it monstrously ef my rifle had tuck down the good old chap."[10]

Meanwhile, Union General Edwin Sumner's II Army Corps had been massing at Fairfax Court House to assist Pope if need be, but primarily to secure the routes of retreat back to the capital. "Retiring on Washington" was how the Union soldiers delicately phrased it. Men and mules were thoroughly exhausted. All were mud-splattered, lying and standing everywhere, with thousands of little fires glowing within the open fields around Fairfax Courthouse.[11] So when the time came to move out, General Oliver O. Howard was placed in charge of the rear guard and promptly ordered the 1st Minnesota of Willis Gorman's brigade and the 19th Massachusetts regiment of General Napoleon Dana's brigade out to the north of town to act as the skirmish line covering the rear guard of the entire column. The Minnesotans had been on the field since the 30th and were called together shortly after noon. A general inspection was given of the men and their weaponry. Soon after, all those deemed unfit for another night march were sent on with the rest of the brigade, leaving only about three hundred men fit for rear-guard duty. They were coupled with a section of Battery A of the First Rhode Island artillery, with orders to stay on the outskirts of Fairfax till nightfall, and then follow the rest of the brigades, covering the Vienna Road along the way.[12]

By contrast, the 19th had left Washington at 2:00 A.M. that morning and had marched west from the capital in drenching rain and thick mud. Bemoaning the fact they didn't even have time to make coffee, the wet and exhausted Bay Staters watched the massive blue line snake its way eastward along the Flint Hill and Vienna Road which in turn would take them to the Potomac's Chain Bridge crossing and into the safety of the capital.[13]

Any seasoned veteran knew what rear-guard positioning meant to their likelihood of seeing action. The Union men fully expected harassing attacks from the Confederate cavalry. This day was no exception and it was not long in coming. Finally arriving at Flint Hill near dusk, Stuart's artillerists opened the action by lobbing a few shells at part of the Federal rear guard that was retreating northward through Vienna. While the horse artillery was doing its work, Stuart's riders thundered off to the Confederate left to badger the flank of the quickly withdrawing Federals. This initial barrage sent the bluecoats scurrying and created panic amongst the horses pulling the wagons and ambulances. The Confederate aim was true, for the 19th Massachusetts was obliged to move several times its length while under direct fire to seek out a safer position, carrying out the movement with skill and confidence. General Howard later noted of the 19th, "the coolness and perfect quietness and absence of any hurry or confusion was most gratifying to see."[14]

Sensing that he had them on the run, Stuart pounded forward with his aide, Heros von Borcke, to survey the scene from the ridge line. His view was one of intense fires blazing throughout the near empty town, while trooper James Moore of the 2nd Virginia cavalry observed how the buildings "glared up fiercely in the twilight gloom." Though it was impossible to tell from the distance whether it was commissary stores or citizens' homes that were enflamed, Stuart was nevertheless convinced that his enemy was engaged in wanton destruction of civilian property. Fully enraged, Stuart growled at von Borcke, "Major, ride as quick as you can, and bring up some of [Captain William] Pelham's guns at full gallop, that we may give a parting salute to these rascally incendiaries."[15]

By now, the Union men were able to set up a few guns and infantry of their own in the surrounding woods to return the fire, however. The Confederates prepared to regroup and press the attack, though this time the Minnesotans, their comrades from Massachusetts, and Tompkin's Rhode Island battery set a trap for the approaching horsemen atop Flint Hill. Advance pickets were sent to skirmish about one hundred fifty yards from the hidden main line. "It was understood that we were to be sacrificed....Our firing was to give notice to the regiment that the enemy was upon us. Each man took his tree and in a few minutes his cavalry and a battery appeared."[16]

John Reynolds of the 19th Massachusetts observed that "Sitting on my horse and looking down the road, we could distinctly see the encounter between our mounted pickets and the enemy as they came on." Slowly and intentionally, the 19th backed up Flint Hill along the rough road, the discharge of the carbines telling all that the rebels were approaching. Reynolds continued: "Now and then a horse, with his empty saddle galloped along the road toward us, showing that his rider had been killed or wounded."[17] When Stuart's troopers were close enough, the trap was sprung. A Minnesotan portrayed the ambush, "Two guns stood in the middle of the road near the top of the [Flint] hill,[18] and the wings of the regiment were, on either side, thrown forward, forming the letter 'V', so as to partly envelop the approaching foe. Silently we waited, but not for long, for the rebel cavalry and artillery, finding the road clear, hurried on in pursuit, not discovering us until the advance was nearly at the muzzles of our guns. [Colonel] Sully's challenge, 'Who comes there?' and the surprised response, 'Who the devil are you?' and a pistol-shot from the rebel leader directed at Sully brought a volley of cannister from the two pieces and musketry from the First Minnesota, which must have done fearful execution, judging from the cries, groans, curses and commands, as those who were able dashed madly to the rear, hastened by a second volley from the guns and the regiment, and during the night they troubled us no more."[19] Private James Groat of the 1st Minnesota wrote: "We gave them a volley of minnies, and shot and shell from our cannon. The enemy was thrown into the utmost confusion and ran panic stricken like scared rabbits."[20] Quickly deciding that this probe was not turning out the way they hoped, the Confederate cavalry broke off and withdrew from Flint Hill, though some elements of Stuart's cavalry would continue to harass the bluecoats as far east as Annandale.[21] Confederate accounts admitted the loss of only one man, though Private Groat claimed in his diary that rebel killed and wounded were about thirty. "This engagement," Groat proclaimed, "the old First called the Battle of Flint Hill."[22]

Cheers erupted along the Union line, but the Yankee hurrahs quickly turned to groans for both regiments on the ensuing march back to their column. After ensuring that the rebel horsemen had in fact departed, General Howard rode with his orderlies back to the two regiments ordering them to find their way back to the rest of the corps. The 1st Minnesota was in the lead and upon its arrival just outside of the little village of Vienna was wrongly assumed by the main body to be the entire rear guard.[23] The 9th New York cavalry, now night patrolling in the area, mistakenly believed the returning skirmishers were Confederates and ordered a charge through the ranks. Since the unfortunate attack came from their new front, both the 1st and 19th immediately knew a horrible mistake was unfolding. Minnesotan Edward Walker wrote, "We of course thought we had run into a nest of guerrillas and some of our men returned the fire." A stampede ensued with both men and horses running who knew where until the mistake became clear and order was restored. Walker continued, "It was all over in no time and soon discovered that all belonged to our army, and that there was no Secesh near."[24]

The Union march through Fairfax County to Alexandria and Washington continued unimpeded through the remainder of the evening thereby allowing Stuart's shaken troopers to ride proudly that night into the village of Fairfax Court House. With the departure of their Union occupiers, the Fairfax citizenry gave Stuart and his horsemen a hero's welcome and it was here that they bivouacked the night of September 2.[25] The net result of the day's action for Stuart's men was the capture of about forty prisoners and fifteen wagons.

Modern view of the original Fairfax Court House

Collection of the author

Apparently, most of these wagons were Union ambulances that were en route to the Bull Run battlefield to pick up Union wounded. Robert E. Lee was advised of the capture, and when learning of the wagons' purposes, Lee had them released and allowed to continue on their mission of mercy.[26]

Some Confederate prisoners had also been released by the Yankees at Fairfax, believing that with the Union withdrawal, the prisoners' Confederate brethren would move in to find them. Amongst them was Parson Landstreet of General Jeb Stuart's family church, released specifically to give Stuart a special offer from John Pope. It seemed that in the days before both Pope's coat and Stuart's hat had been either stolen by the enemy or otherwise lost to their owners. Pope's message was straightforward. If Stuart would send him back his coat, he would return him his hat! Stuart would have none of it. The hat had to come back first. After the wholesale destruction and death of the preceding five days, there was still energy for light-hearted human contact amongst military brothers.[27]

By the time dusk arrived on the evening of September 2, Lee realized that Pope was long gone, that his flanking opportunity had been lost, and that it would not be prudent to try smashing through the capital's heavily defended outer works. Lee later reported to Confederate President Jefferson Davis that "The enemy conducted his retreat so rapidly that the attempt to intercept him was abandoned."[28]

**Jedediah Hotchkiss,
Stonewall Jackson's
cartographer**
Library of Congress

Attention turned to burying of the dead, helping find wounded comrades, and to decide on the next move. Rounding up stragglers was a concern as well, and they were everywhere. Confederate cartographer Jed Hotchkiss had ridden westward on the 2nd to the small village of Aldie to procure a map of Virginia's Loudoun County in preparation of the army's next move, and observed that he saw gray- and butternut-clad men wandering everywhere.[29] Union stragglers arriving in Washington reported that "the rebels assisted the men in the burial of our dead...whom they stripped of their clothing with the exception of their pants....the [rebels] at the time were so hungry that they rushed for the haversacks of our killed and wounded."[30]

Prisoners also had to be dealt with. At this stage of the war, the policy for exchanging prisoners was the "parole" system, which had originated in Europe. The system called for captives to give their word not to take up arms against their captors until they were officially exchanged for an enemy prisoner of equal rank. In an era when a man's word and honor were of the highest self-importance, the system worked well until 1863 when Union leaders realized that exchanged prisoners were making up the highest level of new inductees into the Confederate army. Parole was supposed to take place within ten days of capture. Generally, it was granted within a few days, especially after a major battle where thousands of troops were involved. Such was the case after Manassas and Chantilly where scores of men had to be exchanged. Union prisoners were facing the prospects of even less rations than their Confederate captors. Isaac Rathbun of the 86th New York recorded in his diary that through the "generosity" of the rebels, he and his comrades received two crackers apiece. With lulls in the fighting finally at hand, the soldiers and their prisoners often exchanged civil, if not exactly friendly, conversation. The New Yorker went on observing that many rebels had stated that they wished the war were over but would fight on forever if need be before allowing themselves to be subjugated by the Yankees: "They seemed to think we were fighting for Negroes or something else while they were fighting for their homes."[31]

The Confederates were no doubt humored due to a different type of prisoner they were holding in their ranks. In anticipation of the huge battle that had brewed several days before on the old Bull Run battlefield, and in similar fashion to the first battle a year before on that same ground, a number of Northern citizens from Washington had gone out to the battlefield expecting "to see the rebels run," according to one Georgian. It didn't happen. Having ventured too far into the battle area, these men were captured and rounded up by rebel cavalry units along with scores of straggling men in blue. The bemused Georgia private sarcastically continued in his diary: "To their utter astonishment they came in contact with old Stonewall, who took the proper care of them. I saw about seventy-five of them. They were decidedly the cheapest looking set I ever beheld."[32] Sharing those sentiments was a rebel artillerist, who, having an eye to the morrow wryly remarked that "This sample of gentleman of leisure gave us an idea of the material the North had in reserve, to be utilized, if need be, in the future."[33]

Lee decided that a new plan of action was called for. With his troops weary, ragged, and hungry, plus northern Virginia farmland desolated by over a year of heavy fighting, Lee, flush with success from Second Manassas, decided to venture for the first time into Maryland, to take the war to the North, now that Virginia was cleared of a Union presence. Lee wrote: "The great advantage of the advance of the army is the withdrawal of the enemy from our territory and the hurling back upon their capital their two great armies from the banks of the James and Rappahannock rivers."[34] General Daniel H. Hill's division had now arrived from the Shenandoah Valley, in so doing giving Lee approximately 70,000 men to work with. Though Lee knew his army as a whole was dead tired, hungry, and in need of provisions, he felt delay would be costly. On September 3 he wrote to Jefferson Davis, saying, in part: "The army is not properly equipped for an invasion of an enemy's territory. It lacks much of the material of war, is feeble in transportation, the animals being much reduced, and the men are poorly provided with clothes, and in thousands of instances are destitute of shoes. Still, we cannot afford to be idle, and though weaker than our opponents in men and military equipments, must endeavor to harass if we cannot destroy them. I am aware that the movement is attended with much risk, yet I do not consider success impossible, and shall endeavor to guard it from loss. As long as the army of the enemy are employed on this frontier I have no fears for the safety of Richmond...."[35]

The day after Ox Hill, Lee issued orders for his army to march northwest toward Leesburg, but by way of Dranesville, to give the allusion of yet another threat to the capital. Once again, tight-lipped secrecy was Jackson's order of the day. "No one knows anything that is to be done except our generals," wrote a South Carolinian in a letter home. Longstreet's men fared little better regarding plans. "We could gain no news as to our destination and traveled through byroads for miles...until we met General Jackson's forces," a surgeon recorded who was part of Ol' Pete's wing.[36] Once outside of Leesburg, Lee's army was placed where it would be easiest to cross the Potomac into Maryland.[37] By September 5, his ragged legions would be crossing the Potomac at White's Ford, just below the Point of Rocks,[38] however many of those rebels who were barefoot would be ordered to stay behind on the south side of that river.[39]

Federal alarm regarding the safety of the capital was understandable, given the severity of the military defeats they had recently endured. A lack of intelligence regarding Confederate intentions added to the panic, with many expecting an imminent rebel attack on Washington. Arsenal stores were ordered evacuated, and a Federal warship stood at the ready to carry Lincoln and the cabinet to safety if need be. In addition, the military governor of Washington wanted to ensure panic did not break out within the anxiety-ridden populace, so as of the 3rd he ordered all taverns closed. The *Washington Star* reported that the order was "designed to meet the emergency of the present excited state of our population, already worked up to a high pitch by our recent battles, without the addition of liquid stimulus."[40] General George McClellan at his headquarters in Alexandria, Virginia, felt compelled to advise his wife that he did not regard Washington as safe, but that "If I can quietly slip over there, I will send your silver off...."[41]

Secretary of the Navy Gideon Welles was one of the few who correctly predicted in his diary what would play out. "The military believe a great and decisive battle to be fought in front of our city, but I do not anticipate it...perhaps they may venture to cross the upper Potomac...they will not venture to come here, where we are prepared and fortified with both army and navy to meet them."[42]

In reality, both the Union and Confederate armies had had enough for the time being. Federal troops streamed east up the gently rolling hills of the Warrenton Pike through mud knee-deep in places, through Fairfax Court House, and then into the safety of the Washington defenses, many of them looking as beat up as they no doubt felt.[43] "Our uniforms at this time would have disgraced a beggar. Our pants had worn away so much that they hardly reached the knee, and the bottoms were in tatters. Our overcoats were not much better, being burnt here and there in the skirts, by laying too near the fire. The whole uniform being pretty well stained up with mud and ashes."[44] One Union private wrote in a letter home on September 3 that he and his comrades had worn their shirts for three weeks in a row without the chance of washing them, and described some of the men as "shoeless ruffians."[45] Union commander John Pope had also had enough. His wire to Henry Halleck early in the morning of September 2 had the tone of an emotionally overwhelmed and defeated man. "I will give battle when I can, but you should come out and see the troops. They were badly demoralized when they joined me, both officers and men, and there is an intense idea among them that they must get behind the entrenchments....You had best at once decide what is to be done. The enemy is in very heavy force and must be stopped in some way. These forces under my command are not able to do so in the open field, and if again checked I fear the force will be useless afterwards."[46] Halleck tersely responded to Pope that "You will bring your forces as best you can within or near the line of fortification. General McClellan has charge of all the defenses, and you will consider any direction, as to disposition of the troops as they arrive, given by him as coming from me. Do not let the enemy get between you and the works. It is impossible for me to leave Washington."[47]

At 4:00 P.M. on September 2, George McClellan and his staff rode out to the furthermost capital defenses at Upton's Hill, near Alexandria, to meet the downtrodden legions. John Pope and his top lieutenant, Irvin McDowell, rode at the head of their columns with their staff officers as McClellan approached. Years later, McClellan wrote in his memoirs of the approaching party: "I never saw a more helpless-looking headquarters....He [Pope] could give me no information of any importance in relation to the whereabouts of the different corps, except in a most indefinite way; had evidently not troubled his head in the slightest about the movements of his army in retreat, and had coolly preceded the troops, leaving them to get out of the scrape as best they could."[48] General Jacob Cox, who was with McClellan, recalled the tragic encounter: "Their uniforms and that of all the party was covered with dust, their beards were covered with it; they looked worn and serious, but alert and self-possessed...both parties bowed, and the cavalcade moved on. [General John] Hatch was present near Pope, when McClellan assumed command, and instantly rode a few paces to the head of his column and shouted, 'Boys, McClellan is in command again; three cheers!' The cheers were given in wild delight, and were taken up and passed toward the rear of the column. Warm friend of McClellan as I was, I felt my flesh cringe at the unnecessary affront to the commander of that army. But no word was spoken. Pope lifted his hat in a parting salute to McClellan and rode quietly on with his escort." McClellan never saw Pope again.[49]

Clearly, many of the foot soldiers had had their fill of John Pope as well. A Wisconsin private disdainfully remarked that Pope had the army "scattered from Hell to breakfast," and that the rebs had taken full advantage of the gaffe.[50] Another McClellanite soldier delighted in a typically anti-Pope letter that "...his [Pope] jealous slurs of McClellan have recoiled on himself. He is done for, and now even Greeley[51] admits that McClellan's 'mud digging' has been the salvation of Washington."[52] Nor were the concern and anger limited to the privates. Colonel Orlando Poe, whose Third Brigade under Kearny had held the field and then the rear guard at Chantilly, wrote to his wife on September 4: "I believe that the war is nearly over, for the enemy is an audacious one, and we are not going to be allowed to take our ease here."[53]

The feeling of demoralization was pronounced, especially in the letters of soldiers to their families and to their hometown newspapers, many of which simply stated that nothing positive would occur until a change in command at the top was effected. So great was the angst that the heavily Democratic *New York World* editorialized, "The letters received from our soldiers, officers and privates, since the late battles, are not pitched in the right key. They show demoralization and want of heart from the wretched management in the late encounters," and urged its readership to send uplifting letters back to their men.[54]

With the stroke of a pen on September 7, Secretary of War Edwin Stanton issued General Orders #128, dismissing Pope from command as he had requested, and sending him to Minnesota as titular head of the Department of the Northwest. His sole task at his new, self-described "remote and unimportant command" would be to keep the Sioux Indians at bay, thereby effectively ending his Civil War military career.[55] Within three weeks the Union Army of Virginia would cease to exist, as it would be merged into the Union Army of the Potomac. The new commander would once again be thirty-five-year-old George McClellan, staunch Democrat and political foe of the radical and abolitionist Republicans, much to the raucous delight of his Army of the Potomac soldiers. Lincoln was convinced that McClellan was lacking as an offensive-minded general, who suffered from the "slows" and was "good for nothing for an onward movement," as Lincoln put it.[56] He, as well as members of his cabinet, led by Secretary of War Edwin Stanton and Secretary of the Treasury Salmon P. Chase, also had a keen mistrust of McClellan's motives, believing that he had wanted to see Pope defeated, in light of McClellan's wire to "leave Pope to get out of his scrape."[57] Chase was especially livid, writing in his diary that "Giving McClellan back the command was like giving Washington to the rebels." In fact, the cabinet's hesitation and suspicions were probably not far off the mark. George McClellan was no admirer of John Pope's; on August 8 he had written to his wife remarking on Pope's earlier orders for dealing with the Virginia citizenry that "I will not permit *this army* [Army of the Potomac] to degenerate into a mob of thieves, nor will I return these men of mine to their families as a set of wicked & demoralized robbers." Two days later he predicted to his wife that "I have a very strong idea that Pope will be thrashed during the coming week—& very badly whipped he will be & ought to be—such a villain as he is ought to bring defeat upon any cause that employs him...."[58] Of further chagrin to Lincoln was his belief that Halleck's orders to McClellan of the past week to bring up elements of the Army of the Potomac to assist Pope were not carried out by McClellan with the haste that the government intended. Nevertheless, George McClellan was given back the command by default. "We must use what tools we have," spoke Lincoln, and then referring to McClellan, stated that there was simply "no man in the army who can man these fortifications and lick these troops of ours into shape half as well as he."[59] Lincoln was right, for though no words were recorded between the two as to the shape of the army, they both were well aware that McClellan had his hands full with reenergizing the boys in blue. John Whiteside of the 105th New York keenly observed in a letter home that "We were now greatly demoralized. Neither men nor officers had any spirit to march and had but very little disposition to fight. This was obvious to any military man from the fact that straggling was the order of the day. We were marched to death."[60]

McClellan's public acceptance of the new command was false humility. Privately, in letters to his wife, he was ecstatic, especially in light of Henry Halleck's fervent plea of the 31st, "I beg of you to assist me in this crisis with your ability and experience. I am utterly tired out."[61] To his wife, Mary, on the fifth he wrote, "Again I have been called upon to save the country...." and on the seventh, "I now have the entire confidence of the Govt & love of this army—my enemies are crushed, silent & disarmed—if I defeat the rebels, I shall be master of the situation...."[62]

On the Confederate side, Lee was, of course, disinterested in Federal politics and would have his own fish to fry. His plan would be to crush the Federal army out in the open, which Lee correctly reasoned would have to follow him into the North. Once destroyed, he could move eastward striking Baltimore, Harrisburg, or even Washington, "as the opportunity may present itself."

With its rout of Pope's Federal forces at Second Manassas and its coda at Chantilly, the Confederacy was now in a ten-month period that would be its military zenith, the forthcoming strategic loss at Sharpsburg notwithstanding. In a span of merely two months, Robert E. Lee and his ragged legions had driven two immense Union armies from the outskirts of Richmond all the way back into the entrenchments of Washington, D.C. Both sides now stood essentially where they were when the war first started. Forevermore, Robert E. Lee, "Stonewall" Jackson, and Jeb Stuart would reside in the pantheon of Confederate mythology.

Major events in history often turn on small, seemingly inconsequential moments, and this first of three Confederate attempts to carry the war into the North would likewise turn, two weeks later, with a small, discarded piece of paper tied to three cigars, found by two Union soldiers in a Maryland field...

EPILOGUE

The Battlefield Area Today

It should be noted that the modern, twenty-first-century town of Chantilly in Fairfax County, Virginia, is centered near the intersection of modern Route 50 and Route 28. This is approximately one to two miles west of Civil War-era Chantilly, which referenced not a town but rather a stately mansion of the day and its surrounding area. Ox Hill is the topographical rise primarily at the intersection of modern Route 50 (Lee-Jackson Highway) and West Ox Road. As we start the new millennium, the area where the Battle of Ox Hill occurred has become a "lost battlefield," according to the 1991 Congressional Civil War Sites Advisory Commission. The Reid and Milan houses are gone, as is the cornfield and woods where such vicious hand-to-hand fighting occurred. Sadly, in fact, virtually every square foot of the nineteenth-century battlefield is covered by modern development, from strip shopping malls to row upon row of contemporary town homes. In many cases, the construction of these buildings altered the topography of the land. The Civil War-era Ox Road is known today as West Ox Road, and follows roughly the same path as it did during the war. What was then a thin, single-laned dirt road is today a bustling six to eight lane behemoth whose widening and upgrade, however, resulted in a significant elevating from its original single lane days. Road construction over the past three decades also resulted in the pinnacle of Ox Hill being flattened to allow for the construction of bridges. The net result to today's visitor is that the slope of Ox Hill is not nearly as pronounced at it would have appeared during the battle. Off to the east, the Difficult Run streambed is all but invisible to visitors. Construction of Interstate 66 in the 1960s and the concurrent bridge construction of Modern Route 50 *(Little River Turnpike)* have placed the small stream practically out of view and even existence.

All that remains is a 4.5-acre county park *(Ox Hill Battlefield Park)* at the center of the battlefield *(at the modern intersection of Monument Avenue and West Ox Road)*, where the early twentieth-century monuments to the memory of Generals Kearny and Stevens may be found. A visitor to the park should not be confused in thinking that these side-by-side monuments mark the spots where the generals fell. Though Stevens' point of death is considered at or very close to the monuments, it is generally agreed that Kearny's mortal wound occurred at least 150 to 200 yards to the south and west of the monuments.

The park itself presents a tranquil visit to the visitor, however tree and foliage growth over the years within the park have rendered it historically inaccurate compared to its wartime appearance. An encouraging sign to rectify this exists at the time of this writing, as there is talk within Fairfax County to restore the ground to its Civil War form, including possible placement of a snake-rail fence and a small cornfield where possible.

The Kearny and Stevens monuments present a unique history. An interesting contemporary newspaper account of the dedication of these monuments follows: "It was my good fortune to attend a very interesting ceremony recently (October 2), which was the unveiling and dedication of markers showing where Gens. Phil Kearny and Isaac Stevens, of the Federal army, were killed in the battle of Chantilly (Ox Hill) on September 1, 1862. On this occasion there were quite a number of G. A. R.[1] men present and also many who had worn the gray. There was much good feeling shown, and upon inquiry I learned that the plot of ground, one-fourth of an acre, for these markers, had been donated to the Kearny Commission, of New Jersey, for this purpose by a gallant ex-Confederate who had left one limb on some other battle field. The Jersey men seemed to appreciate greatly the fact that this ex-Confederate had kept this spot marked all these years, thus showing the admiration that one brave man feels for another. This Confederate veteran was John N. Ballard, who was one of Mosby's men and who followed that gallant leader until the close of the war."[2]

How the virtually complete destruction of this Civil War battlefield came to pass is a story in itself, being what became known to

John N. Ballard as a young man during the war

Fairfax Herald

local preservationists as the "Battle of Second Chantilly." As early as the mid-1980s it became known to local Civil War preservationists that key elements of the battlefield, then forest and open ground, were slated to be bulldozed to make way for a shopping center, roads, and town homes. The new construction would be located at the epicenter of the battlefield, including the cornfield. Prior to this time, organized civilian interest in protecting the battlefield was next to nil, and official public policy, both local and state, regarding this hallowed ground was nonexistent. A 1979 letter from the Fairfax County Board of Supervisors to the U.S. Secretary of the Interior proposing that the National Park Service study the desirability of acquiring park land to save the battlefield garnered no interest, and as late as 1986, this site of the largest Civil War battle in Fairfax County did not even appear on the county's historic tour maps.[3] When the developer's plans became known, attempts were made to fight the changes in the county's master zoning plan that led to the developer's decision to build there in the first place. County supervisors argued, however, that those changes were only made after "considerable input" from Fairfax residents. Fairfax County's pro-development stance, coupled with the lack of public outcry, ultimately doomed preservationists' efforts. "It was like trying to throw Jello against the wall," said Kim Holien, historian at the U.S. Army Center of Military History. "You just literally got no response."[4] Once the bulldozers began their work, the inevitable uncovering of graves and artifacts began, to the dismay of all concerned. The remains of a South Carolinian soldier were discovered, which were sent back to South Carolina to be reburied with full military honors. A courageous rallying cry was put forth and much wrangling went on, with the saving of the small, aforementioned park the net result. The developer graciously offered to donate a small parcel of land if Fairfax County would purchase an adjacent area and donate it as well.

Long-term benefits to the preservation cause were borne out of "2nd Chantilly" as well, as it served as a wake-up call that formal organization to preserve Civil War battlefields was needed. From the loss at Chantilly, the Association for the Preservation of Civil War Sites (APCWS) was born, having merged in 1999 with the Civil War Trust to form the *Civil War Preservation Trust*, dedicated to preventing another "Second Chantilly." Though this field of honor is gone, its loss has helped save thousands of other priceless acres of our heritage.

Early twentieth-century view of the Kearny-Stevens monuments
Note the wide open, still-pristine battlefield in the background.
Fairfax County and the War Between the States

Modern view of the Kearny-Stevens monuments
Steven's division would have charged up the sloping ground towards the camera.
Collection of the author

APPENDIX 1

Union General Isaac Ingalls Stevens

Stevens was born March 25, 1818, at Andover, Massachusetts. After graduating first in his class at the West Point Military Academy, Stevens fought in the Mexican War, and was then posted to what was then called the Oregon Territory. The vast area—stretching west of Missouri Territory and north of California and New Mexico—included what is now Oregon, Washington, Idaho, and roughly half of Montana. He was then appointed governor at age thirty-five, and remains today as the youngest governor in Washington history. One of the most notable and important accomplishments while in office was his negotiation of peace treaties with numerous Native American tribes. Following his term as governor, he served in Congress from 1857 to 1861.

When the Union forces were defeated at the first battle of Manassas, Stevens offered his services to the Federal government. Unfortunately, due to his prior political activities, there was little excitement within Secretary of War Simon Cameron's offices for making a general of Stevens. However, the realization by the Union command that the Civil War was going to last far longer than initially thought, resulted in a change of his fortune. Stevens was made a colonel commanding the 79th New York Infantry regiment, also known as "the Highlanders" due to the large number of Scotsmen in the regiment.

Assumption of command quickly brought a crisis to Colonel Stevens—mutiny within the regiment due to a rumor that no leave would be granted to the troops. The mutiny broke out as situations between the old command and Stevens came to a head, and Federal assistance was required to end the revolt.

Soon, Colonel Stevens' ability to lead was recognized and he was given command of a brigade in General Smith's division. Then followed a transfer to command of the Second Brigade of the Expeditionary Corps, responsible for leading a combined forces attack on the Sea Islands off South Carolina's coast. One of the most bitter moments of Stevens' command came during June 1862 at Secessionville, a battle that was supposed to be the attempt to secure Charleston. Secessionville, known as Fort Lamar to the Confederacy, was a fortification on James Island. Stevens was ordered to lead an assault on the fortifications. In the attack, Stevens lost 25 percent of his division, including numerous men from the 79th Highlanders. While Stevens took pride in the gallantry of his Highlanders, he found himself being blamed by his superior, General Henry Benham, for the failed attack. Washington paid little attention to Benham's accusations, and he was ultimately dismissed that August.

In July, Stevens' men were ordered north to join the IX Corps of the Army of Potomac in Virginia. In August, Stevens' division was ordered by General John Pope to Cedar Mountain. On August 24, 1862, the general's troops were involved in a skirmish at Sulphur Springs, and at the battle of Second Bull Run on August 28–30, 1862. Stevens was promoted to brigadier general on September 28, 1861, and was promoted posthumously to major general. Stevens County, Washington, is named for him. His son, Hazard, wrote a history of Washington, as well as a two-volume history of his father's life.

APPENDIX 2

Union General Philip Kearny

Philip Kearny was born June 2, 1815, in New York. He spent the bulk of his youth under the care of his maternal grandfather who was a man of wealth and high social prominence. Kearny's uncle, General Stephen Watts Kearny, was a U.S. dragoon and had a profound effect upon Philip's future choice of the military as a career. His grandfather, though, discouraged it and urged the young Kearny instead to seek academia.

Upon graduating from Columbia University in 1833, Kearny traveled widely. When his grandfather died, leaving him an estate valued at a million dollars, he returned home, and in 1837 obtained a commission as second lieutenant in the 1st U.S. Dragoons. After two years service with them, the secretary of war sent him to the French Cavalry School at Saumur to study cavalry tactics. While there, Kearny saw action in Algiers, serving with the Chasseurs d'Afrique.

On his return to the U.S. in the early 1840s, he served as aide-de-camp to, successively, Alexander Macomb and Winfield Scott, generals in chief of the army. In the Mexican War, Kearny was involved in the battles of Contreras and Churubusco, and at the end of the latter, led his own dragoons on a successful charge into Mexico City. Here, he was shot in the left arm, it being so damaged that the arm had to be amputated. He was brevetted major for gallantry and, after service in California, resigned from the army in 1851, married, and made his home in Belle Grove, New Jersey. The military attracted him again in 1859, when he served in Napoleon III's Imperial Guard in the Italian War, winning the French Legion of Honor for bravery at Solferino. In 1861, soon after the beginning of the Civil War, Kearny returned to the United States to offer his services. He was among the first brigadier generals of volunteers appointed (August 7 to rank from May 17, 1861) and was assigned to command the 1st Brigade of New Jersey militia regiments under General William B. Franklin's division of the Army of the Potomac. During the Peninsula Campaign he was present at the Battle of Williamsburg where his timely arrival changed the Confederate repulse into Union victory.

When Union General Oliver O. Howard lost his right arm at the Battle of Fair Oaks, Kearny happened to be present when the amputation was performed and, Howard looking up, said: "We'll buy our gloves together hereafter."

One of the best known and respected soldiers in the army, he distinguished himself all through the Peninsula Campaign, rising to major general to command of the 1st Division of Major General Samuel P. Heintzelman's III Corps at the time of Second Manassas and Ox Hill.

APPENDIX 3

The Kearny Patch and Medal

Another key issue of historical military importance arose directly from the battle of Ox Hill. Prior to his death, General Philip Kearny had ordered that the officers and men under his command would wear a special badge so that they would be known to each other wherever they met. This badge was to be a piece of cloth, worn on the cap or hat, and was to be visible at all times. Three days after the battle at Chantilly, General David Birney, now in command of the division by virtue of his seniority, decreed that all officers in the division would wear crepe on their arms for thirty days and that the colors and drums of the regiments and batteries would be placed in mourning for sixty days. He then followed through on Kearny's order by declaring that the officers would also wear a piece of scarlet cloth on their cap. The patch soon took the form of a diamond and became known as the "Kearny Patch."

On November 29, 1862 , a number of officers who served with him gathered together to formally honor the fallen leader. At the meeting a resolution was adopted that a medal of honor would be created, to be known as the "Kearny Medal" and that it would be awarded to all officers who had "honorably served in battle under General Kearny in his division." Joseph Hooker, now in command of the Army of the Potomac expanded this notion in early January 1863 such that each corps would now have its own identifying badge. Then, on March 13, 1863, Birney issued an order to the effect that a "Cross of Valor," to be known as the "Kearny Cross," would be awarded to noncommissioned officers and privates who had "most distinguished themselves in battle." These concepts of unique badges to identify units, and an award of valor to those men who distinguished themselves beyond the call of duty would eventually evolve into today's standard practice of corps identity, both concepts tracing their roots to the battle of Chantilly.[1]

APPENDIX 4

Order of Battle at Ox Hill[1]

UNION ARMY

MAJOR GENERAL JOHN POPE, COMMANDING

<u>Third Corps, Army of the Potomac</u>

MAJOR GENERAL SAMUEL P. HEINTZELMAN

First Division
MAJOR GENERAL PHILIP KEARNY (killed at Ox Hill)

First Brigade
BRIGADIER GENERAL JOHN C. ROBINSON

20th Indiana Infantry Regiment
63rd Pennsylvania Infantry Regiment
105th Pennsylvania Infantry Regiment

Second Brigade
BRIGADIER GENERAL DAVID B. BIRNEY

3rd Maine Infantry Regiment
4th Maine Infantry Regiment
1st New York Infantry Regiment
38th New York Infantry Regiment
40th New York Infantry Regiment
101st New York Infantry Regiment
57th Pennsylvania Infantry Regiment

Third Brigade
COLONEL ORLANDO M. POE

2nd Michigan Infantry Regiment
3rd Michigan Infantry Regiment
5th Michigan Infantry Regiment
37th New York Infantry Regiment
99th Pennsylvania Regiment

Artillery

Battery E, 1st Rhode Island Artillery
Battery K, 1st U.S. Artillery

IX Corps, Army of the Potomac

MAJOR GENERAL JESSE L. RENO[2]

First Division
BRIGADIER GENERAL ISAAC I. STEVENS (killed at Ox Hill)

First Brigade
COLONEL BENJAMIN C. CHRIST

8th Michigan Infantry Regiment
50th Pennsylvania Infantry Regiment

Second Brigade
COLONEL DANIEL LEASURE[3]

46th New York Infantry Regiment (5 Companies)
100th Pennsylvania Infantry Regiment

Third Brigade
COLONEL ADDISON FARNSWORTH[4]

28th Massachusetts Infantry Regiment
79th New York Infantry Regiment

Second Division
MAJOR GENERAL JESSE L. RENO

First Brigade
COLONEL JAMES NAGLE

2nd Maryland Infantry Regiment
48th Pennsylvania Infantry Regiment

6th New Hampshire Infantry Regiment
9th New Hampshire Infantry Regiment

Second Brigade
COLONEL EDWARD FERRERO

21st Massachusetts Infantry Regiment
51st New York Infantry Regiment
51st Pennsylvania Infantry Regiment

CONFEDERATE ARMY

MAJOR GENERAL ROBERT E. LEE, COMMANDING

Second Corps, Army of Northern Virginia, aka "Left Wing"

MAJOR GENERAL THOMAS "STONEWALL" JACKSON

First Division
BRIGADIER GENERAL WILLIAM E. STARKE[5]

First Brigade "Stonewall Brigade" aka "Winder's Brigade"[6]
COLONEL A. J. GRIGSBY

2nd Virginia Infantry Regiment
4th Virginia Infantry Regiment
5th Virginia Infantry Regiment
27th Virginia Infantry Regiment
33rd Virginia Infantry Regiment

Second Brigade "Campbell's Brigade"
COLONEL BRADLEY T. JOHNSON

21st Virginia Infantry Regiment
42nd Virginia Infantry Regiment
48th Virginia Infantry Regiment
1st Virginia "Irish" Battalion

Third Brigade "Taliaferro's Brigade"
COLONEL ALEXANDER G. TALIAFERRO[7]

47th Alabama Infantry Regiment
48th Alabama Infantry Regiment
10th Virginia Infantry Regiment
23rd Virginia Infantry Regiment
37th Virginia Infantry Regiment

Fourth Brigade "Starke's Brigade"
COLONEL LEROY A. STAFFORD

1st Louisiana Infantry Regiment
2nd Louisiana Infantry Regiment
9th Louisiana Infantry Regiment
10th Louisiana Infantry Regiment
15th Louisiana Infantry Regiment
"Coppens" Louisiana Battalion

First Division Artillery
MAJOR LINDSAY M. SHUMAKER

Maryland Battery—2nd Baltimore Light Artillery
Virginia Battery—Allegheny Artillery
Virginia Battery—Hampden Artillery
Virginia Battery—"Cutshaw's Battery"
Virginia Battery—Rockbridge Artillery
Virginia Battery—Lynchburg "Lee" Artillery
Virginia Battery—Danville Artillery
Virginia Battery—8th Star Artillery
Virginia Battery—Winchester Artillery

2nd (Light) Division
MAJOR GENERAL AMBROSE P. HILL

"Branch's Brigade"
BRIGADIER GENERAL LAWRENCE O'BRYAN BRANCH[8]

7th North Carolina Infantry Regiment
18th North Carolina Infantry Regiment
28th North Carolina Infantry Regiment
33rd North Carolina Infantry Regiment
37th North Carolina Infantry Regiment

"Thomas's Brigade"
COLONEL EDWARD L. THOMAS

14th Georgia Infantry Regiment
35th Georgia Infantry Regiment
45th Georgia Infantry Regiment
49th Georgia Infantry Regiment

"Pender's Brigade"
BRIGADIER GENERAL WILLIAM DORSEY PENDER

16th North Carolina Infantry Regiment
22nd North Carolina Infantry Regiment
34th North Carolina Infantry Regiment
38th North Carolina Infantry Regiment

"Gregg's Brigade"
BRIGADIER GENERAL MAXCY GREGG[9]

1st South Carolina Infantry Regiment
1st South Carolina (Orr) Rifles
12th South Carolina Infantry Regiment
13th South Carolina Infantry Regiment
14th South Carolina Infantry Regiment

"Archer's Brigade"
BRIGADIER GENERAL JAMES J. ARCHER

8th Alabama Infantry Battalion
19th Georgia Infantry Regiment
1st Tennessee Provincial Army
7th Tennessee Infantry Regiment
14th Tennessee Infantry Regiment

"Field's Brigade"
COLONEL JOHN M. BROCKENBROUGH

40th Virginia Infantry Regiment
47th Virginia Infantry Regiment
55th Virginia Infantry Regiment
22nd Virginia Infantry Battalion

2nd Division Artillery
LIEUTENANT COLONEL REUBEN L. WALKER

North Carolina Battery—"Branch" Artillery
South Carolina Battery—"Pee Dee Artillery"
Virginia Battery—Crenshaw Artillery
Virginia Battery—Fredericksburg Artillery
Virginia Battery—Middlesex Artillery
Virginia Battery—Purcell Artillery
Virginia Battery—Letcher Artillery

3rd Division
BRIGADIER GENERAL ALEXANDER R. LAWTON[10]

"Lawton's Brigade"
COLONEL MARCELLUS DOUGLASS[11]

13th Georgia Infantry Regiment
26th Georgia Infantry Regiment
31st Georgia Infantry Regiment
38th Georgia Infantry Regiment
60th Georgia Infantry Regiment
61st Georgia Infantry Regiment

"Trimble's Brigade"
CAPTAIN WILLIAM F. BROWN (killed at Ox Hill)
15th Alabama Infantry Regiment
12th Georgia Infantry Regiment
21st Georgia Infantry Regiment
21st North Carolina Infantry Regiment
1st North Carolina Infantry Battalion

"Early's Brigade"
BRIGADIER GENERAL JUBAL A. EARLY
13th Virginia Infantry Regiment
25th Virginia Infantry Regiment
31st Virginia Infantry Regiment
44th Virginia Infantry Regiment
49th Virginia Infantry Regiment
52d Virginia Infantry Regiment
58th Virginia Infantry Regiment

"Hays' Brigade"
COLONEL HENRY B. STRONG[12]

5th Louisiana Infantry Regiment
6th Louisiana Infantry Regiment
7th Louisiana Infantry Regiment
8th Louisiana Infantry Regiment
14th Louisiana Infantry Regiment

3rd Division Artillery
MAJOR ALFRED R. COURTNEY

Louisiana Battery—"D'Aquin's Guard" Artillery

Maryland Battery—Dement's Artillery
Maryland Battery—Brown's Chesapeake Artillery
Virginia Battery—Johnson's Artillery
Virginia Battery—Courtney Artillery
Virginia Battery—Staunton Artillery

Cavalry Division
MAJOR GENERAL JAMES E. B. STUART

"Robertson's Brigade"
BRIGADIER GENERAL BEVERLY H. ROBERTSON

2d Virginia Cavalry
6th Virginia Cavalry
7th Virginia Cavalry
12th Virginia Cavalry
17th Virginia Cavalry Battalion

"Lee's Brigade"
BRIGADIER GENERAL FITZHUGH LEE

1st Virginia Cavalry
3d Virginia Cavalry
4th Virginia Cavalry
5th Virginia Cavalry
9th Virginia Cavalry

"Hampton's Brigade"[13]
BRIGADIER GENERAL WADE HAMPTON

1st North Carolina Cavalry
2d South Carolina Cavalry
10th Virginia Cavalry
Cobb's (Georgia) Legion Cavalry
Jeff. Davis Legion Cavalry

Cavalry Artillery
South Carolina Battery—Hart's Horse Artillery
Virginia Battery—1st "Stuart" Horse Artillery

NOTES

Chapter 1

1. United States War Department, *The War of the Rebellion: A Compilation of the Official Records of the Union and Confederate Armies,* 128 volumes (Washington D.C., 1881–1902) ser. 1, vol. 12, pt. 3, p. 602. Hereafter referred to as *O.R.;* Brayton Harris, *Blue and Gray in Black and White: Newspapers in the Civil War* (Washington D.C.: Brassey's, 1999), p. 172.

2. George E. Upton, Letter dated September 3, 1862, New Hampshire Historical Society, Concord, N.H.

3. J. Cutler Andrews, *The North Reports the Civil War* (Pittsburgh, Pa.: University of Pittsburgh Press, 1955), pp. 267–68, 697.

4. See endnotes for appendix 4, Order of Battle, for further commentary on who these casualties were.

5. *O.R.* ser. 1, vol. 12, pt. 3, p. 435. In a campaign known to history as the "Peninsula Campaign," General George McClellan and his Army of the Potomac had been battling the Confederates to the east of Richmond since the spring.

6. *O.R.* ser. 1, vol. 12, pt. 2, pp. 50–52.

7. William Blair, *Virginia's Private War: Feeding Body and Soul in the Confederacy, 1861–1865* (New York: Oxford University Press, 1998), p. 79.

8. Clifford Dowdey and Louis Manarin, editors, *The Wartime Papers of R. E. Lee* (Boston: Little, Brown and Co., 1961), p. 240.

9. Dowdey and Manarin. *Wartime Papers...* p. 234. Letter from Robert E. Lee to George McClellan dated July 21, 1862.

10. Lee Report, *O.R.*, ser. 1, vol. 12, pt. 2, p. 176.

11. Dowdey and Manarin, eds. *Wartime Papers...* p. 239. Letter from Robert E. Lee to Thomas J. Jackson dated July 27, 1862.

12. Douglas Southall Freeman, *Lee's Lieutenants: A Study in Command. Vol. 2. Cedar Mountain to Chancellorsville* (New York: Charles Scribners Sons, 1943), p. 33.

13. Ibid., pp. 37–38.

14. Jackson Report, *O.R.*, ser. 1, vol. 12, pt. 2, pp. 183–84.

15. John H. Worsham, *One of Jackson's Foot Cavalry* (New York: Neale Publishing Co., 1912), p. 114.

16. James Wesley Orr, Recollections of the War Between the States, 1861–1865. Personal Papers Collection, The Library of Virginia, Richmond, Va., pp. 8–9.

17. Lawrence L. Hewitt, "A Confederate Foreign Legion: Louisiana 'Wildcats' in the Army of Northern Virginia" in *Journal of Confederate History* (Murfreesboro, Tenn.: Southern Heritage Press, vol. 6): 62. Based upon the memoir of Private William P. Snakenberg, Co. K, 14th Louisiana.

18. William B. Colston, Civil War Recollections. Frederica Trapnell Papers, Virginia Historical Society, p. 16.

19. Douglas Southall Freeman and Grady McWhiney, eds., *Lee's Dispatches: Unpublished Letters of Robert E. Lee, CSA to Jefferson Davis* (New York: G. P. Putnam's, 1957), p. 54.

20. William H. Bolton Family Papers. Letter, September 16, 1862. Virginia Historical Society; John O. Casler, *Four Years in the Stonewall Brigade* (1893; reprint, Dayton: Morningside Press, 1971), p. 107; Alan Gaff, *Brave Men's Tears: The Iron Brigade at Brawner's Farm* (Dayton: Morningside Press, 1985), pp. 24–25.

21. William Frierson Fulton, *Family Record and War Reminiscences* (Ala.: self-published, 1914), p. 69.

22. Orr Recollections, Library of Virginia, p. 9.

23. Casler, p. 108.

24. Elisha Bracken, Diary, July 15, 1862–May 15, 1863. U.S. Army Military History Institute, Carlisle, Pa.

25. *O.R.,* ser. 1, vol. 12, pt. 1, p. 328.

26. McClellan wire, *O.R.,* ser. 1, vol. 11, pt. 1, p. 98.

27. Horatio Belcher, Diary, August 30, 1862, William M. Fenton Collection, Bentley Historical Library, University of Michigan.

28. Daniel Sutherland, *The Emergence of Total War* (Fort Worth: Ryan Place Publishers, 1996), p. 84.

29. Henry Gerrish, *Letter to Lyman* (Springfield, Va.: Genealogical Books In Print, 1978), p. 24.

30. George E. Upton, Letter dated September 3, 1862, New Hampshire Historical Society, Concord, N.H.

31. John Whiteside, Letter dated October 4, 1862, Bentley Historical Library, University of Michigan.

32. Robert Knox Sneden, *Eye of the Storm: A Civil War Odyssey* (New York: The Free Press, 2000), p. 128. Sneden was a private in the 40th New York "Mozart" Regiment.

33. Emil and Ruth Rosenblatt, eds. *Hard Marching Every Day: The Civil War Letters of Private Wilbur Fisk* (Lawrence: University Press of Kansas, 1992), p. 42.

34. United States War Department, *Atlas to Accompany the Official Records of the Union and Confederate Armies,* 2 Vols. (Washington, D.C., 1891–1895), Plates 7 and 111.

Chapter 2

1. Robert E. Lee consistently referred throughout the Civil War to his Union army adversaries as "those people."

2. Asbury Coward [Natalie Bond & Osmun Coward, eds.], *The South Carolinians* (New York: Vantage Press, 1968), p. 53. Coward was the colonel of the 5th South Carolina.

3. James Longstreet, *From Manassas to Appomattox: Memoirs of the Civil War In America* (Philadelphia: Lippincott, 1896), p. 191; *O.R.,* ser. 1, vol. 12, pt. 2, pp. 557–58; D. S. Freeman, *R. E. Lee: A Biography, 4 vols.,* vol. 2 (New York: Charles Scribners Sons, 1934), p. 339.

4. *Philadelphia Daily News,* September 5, 1862; G. Moxley Sorrel, *Recollections of a Confederate Staff Officer* (New York: Smithmark, 1994), pp. 102–3.

5. Report of General James Longstreet, *O.R.,* ser. 1, vol. 12, pt. 2, p. 566.

6. Nicholas Rice, Unpublished Memoir, U.S. Army Military History Institute, Carlisle, Pa., p. 61.

7. Robert Knox Sneden, Memoirs, vol. 3, pt 4. August 30, 1862, to September 15, 1862, p. 608, Virginia Historical Society.

8. James R. Hagood, "Memoirs of the First South Carolina Infantry in the Confederate War For Independence," Manassas National Battlefield Park Library, Manassas, Va., p. 73.

9. Benjamin L. Farinholt, Diary, August 31, 1862. Virginia Historical Society.

10. Andrew C. L. Gatewood, Letter, September 3, 1862. Virginia Military Institute Archives; Draughton S. Haynes, *The Field Diary of a Confederate Soldier* (Darien, Ga.: Ashantilly Press, 1963), p. 14.

11. Henry Kyd Douglas, *I Rode with Stonewall* (Chapel Hill: University of North Carolina, 1940), p. 143.

12. Farinholt Diary, August 31, 1862, Virginia Historical Society.

13. Otto Eisenschiml and Ralph Newman, *Eyewitness: The Civil War as We Lived It* (New York: Grosset and Dunlap, 1956), p. 242.

14. Casler, p. 114.

15. Longstreet, p. 193.

16. William Woods Hassler, *A. P. Hill: Lee's Forgotten General* (Chapel Hill: University of North Carolina, 1962), p. 95.

17. John J. Hennessy, *Return to Bull Run: The Campaign and Battle of Second Manassas* (New York: Simon and Schuster, 1993), p. 49. Original source—William Ellis Jones Diary, August 31, 1862, Clements Library, University of Michigan.

18. William Allan, *Stonewall Jackson, Robert E. Lee, and the Army of Northern Virginia, 1862* (New York: Da Capo Press, 1995), p. 311.

19. John Esten Cooke, *Wearing of the Gray* (Bloomington, Ind.: Indiana University Press, 1959), pp. 212–13. Cooke was a member of General J.E.B. Stuart's staff.

20. Pope wires to Halleck. *O.R.*, ser. 1, vol. 12, pt. 2, pp. 81–83; Hennessy, p. 443.

21. Robert S. Gamble, *Sully: The Biography of a House* (Chantilly: Sully Foundation Ltd., 1973), p. 105.

22. Eleanor Lee Templeman, "Chantilly, Virginia: Historical Highlights" in *The Historical Society of Fairfax County, Virginia Yearbook, Vol. 22, 1989–1990* (Fairfax: Fairfax Historical Society, 1990), p. 120.

23. Alexander Hunter, "A High Privates Account of the Battle of Sharpsburg" in *Southern Historical Society Papers* [hereafter referred to as *SHSP*] vol. 10, nos. 10–11. Richmond, 1884, p. 506. Though long since destroyed, the site of the Chantilly mansion was on State Road 50 about 1/2 mile west of the extant Ayre "stone house," in a small grove of trees between Plum Run Ct. and Tannery Ct. The "stone house" now sits on land owned by the International Town & Country Club,—(Mauro manuscript). The existing Stone House is considered to be the probable residence of Stuart's overseer, and also served as a post office and tavern in the years prior to the war.

24. Elizabeth Brown Pryor, *Walney: Two Centuries of a Northern Virginia Plantation* (Fairfax: Fairfax County Office of History and Archeology, 1984), p. 85; Arthur W. Machen, Jr. *Letters of Arthur W. Machen with Biographical Sketch* (Baltimore: Privately Printed, 1917), pp. 322–23.

25. Douglas, p. 144. Germantown was a small hamlet located near the intersection of modern Routes 50 and 29. Today the general area is referred to as "Jermantown."

26. Captain Thomas Hight report of Sept. 3, 1862, *O.R.*, ser. 1, vol. 12, pt. 3, p. 810; Fitzhugh Lee, *General Lee* (New York: Da Capo Press, 1994), p. 193; Ardyce Kinsley, *The Fitzhugh Lee Sampler* (Privately Printed, 1990), p. 65. Written recollection from one of the Union officers captured by Fitz Lee.

27. Heros von Borcke, *Memoirs of the Confederate War for Independence* (Dayton, Ohio: Morningside, 1985), p. 166.

28. Fitzhugh Lee, pp. 193–94.

29. Report of General J.E.B. Stuart of Cavalry Operations August 30–September 18, 1862. *Southern Historical Society Papers.* vol. 3, p. 28; Munford Report, *O.R.,* ser. 1, vol. 12, pt. 2, p. 749; Cox Report, *O.R.,* ser. 1, vol. 12, pt. 2, pp. 404–5; Noble D. Preston, *History of the Tenth Regiment of Cavalry New York State Volunteers* (New York: D. Appleton & Co., 1892), p. 41.

30. Report of Captain Alfred Tolbert, *O.R.,* ser. 1, vol. 12, pt. 2, p. 538. Tolbert's report totally corroborates the reports of Stuart and von Borcke regarding this affair.

31. R. L. T. Beale, *History of the Ninth Virginia Cavalry* (Richmond, Va.: B. F. Johnson Publishing Co., 1899), p. 36; Stuart, *SHSP*, pp. 281–82.

32. von Borcke, p. 167.

33. Morris Schaff, *The Battle of the Wilderness* (New York: Houghton Mifflin, 1910), p. 319.

34. John G. Moore, "The Battle of Chantilly" in *Military Affairs*, vol. 28, no. 2 (Summer 1964): 53.

35. von Borcke, p. 168.

36. A few remnants of these earthworks still exist, but are rapidly disappearing in the face of modern development.

37. *O.R.,* ser. 1, vol. 12, pt. 2, p. 44; Wilfred W. Thompson, "Campaigns of the 62nd & 155th Pennsylvania Regiments 1861–1865," Bill Worsham Collection, Fairfax, Va.

38. *O.R.,* ser. 1, vol. 12, Supplement, p. 1066.

39. Ibid., p. 81

40. Ibid., p. 79.

41. Henry R. Pyne, *Ride to War: History of the First New Jersey Cavalry* (New Brunswick, N.J.: Rutgers University Press, 1961), pp. 84–85.

42. Horace H. Thomas, "What I Saw Under a Flag of Truce" in *Military Order of the Loyal Legion of the United States* (Hereafter referred to as MOLLUS)—*Illinois,* vol. 10, pt. 1 (Wilmington, N.C.: Broadfoot, 1992), p. 137.

43. Hooker Wire, *O.R.,* ser. 1, vol. 12, pt. 2, p. 437.

44. Stephen Weld, *War Diary and Letters of Stephen Minot Weld* (Boston: Massachusetts Historical Society, 1979), p. 132.

45. Thomas H. Parker, *History of the 51st Regiment of Pennsylvania Volunteers* (Philadelphia: King & Baird, 1869), pp. 218–19; Richard Sauers, ed., *The Civil War Journal of Colonel William J. Bolton, 51st Pennsylvania* (Conshohocken: Combined Publishing, 2000), p. 77.

46. *O.R.* ser. 1, vol. 12, pt. 2, p. 82.

47. Ibid., p. 81.

48. Oliver O. Howard, *Autobiography of Oliver Otis Howard*, vol. 1 (New York: Baker and Taylor Co., 1907), p. 268; Charles H. Banes, *History of the Philadelphia Brigade* (Philadelphia: J. P. Lippincott & Co., 1876), pp. 101–2.

49. *O.R.,* ser. 1, vol. 12, pt. 2, p. 82.

50. M. Shuler, Diary, August 31, 1862, Library of Congress. Shuler was a captain in the 33rd Virginia; W. P. Harper, Diary, August 31, 1862, Manassas National Battlefield Park Library. Harper served with the 7th Louisiana of Hays Brigade. Pleasant Valley is located on modern Route 50 about 1 1/2 miles west of the Route 50 and Route 28 intersection.

51. Douglas Southall Freeman, *Lee's Lieutenants*. vol 2. New York: Scribners, 1942, p. 130; Jedediah Hotchkiss, *Make Me A Map of the Valley: The Civil War Journal of Stonewall Jackson's Topographer* (Dallas, Tex.: Southern Methodist Press, 1973), p. 77.

52. James Richmond Boulware, Diary 1862–1863, Personal Papers Collection, Library of Virginia, Richmond, Va., p. 19. Boulware was an assistant surgeon with the 6th South Carolina.

53. George Wise, *Campaigns and Battles of the Army of Northern Virginia* (New York: Neale, 1916), p. 162. Wise served in Longstreet's 17th Virginia Infantry.

54. Joseph W. A. Whitehorne, "A Beastly, Comfortless Conflict: The Battle Of Chantilly" in *Blue & Gray* 4 (May 1987): 10–11. A fundamental reason for Lee's decision to invade Maryland after Chantilly was to give Virginia's farmlands a reprieve from the ravages of war.

55. Mary Anna Jackson, *Life and Letters of General Thomas J. Jackson* (New York: Harper & Bros., 1892), p. 341.

Chapter 3

1. Early Report, *O.R.,* ser. 1, vol. 12, pt. 2, p. 714.

2. William A. McClendon, *Recollections of War Times, by An Old Veteran, While Under Stonewall Jackson and Lieutenant General James Longstreet; How I Got In and How I Got Out* (Montgomery, Ala.: The Paragon Press, 1909), p. 123.

3. Johnson Report, *O.R.*, ser. 1, vol. 12, pt. 2, p. 667; Pyne, p. 86.

4. George Wise, *History of the 17th Virginia Infantry, C.S.A.* (Baltimore: Kelly, Piet & Co., 1870), p. 105.

5. Tanner, W. R., Sr., in "Reminiscences Of The War Between The States"; available at World Wide Web @ http: members.aol.com/_ht_a/adj61/page3g1.htm ; also text format, Cowpens, S.C.: Privately Printed, 1931. Tanner was a soldier in Co. C, 13th South Carolina.

6. McClendon, p. 123.

7. Robert R. Smith, "The Battle Of Ox Hill" in *Fairfax County and the War Between the States* (Fairfax County Civil War Centennial Commission, Fairfax, Va., 1961), p. 28.

8. Hotchkiss, p. 77.

9. McClendon, p. 123.

10. *O.R.*, ser. 1, vol. 12, pt. 2, p. 667.

11. Until the creation of a man-made refuse mound in the late 1980s, Ox Hill was the highest in Fairfax County, Virginia.

12. Alfred E. Lee, "From Cedar Mountain to Chantilly" in *Magazine of American History,* vol. 16, New York (December 1886), p. 583.

13. William Miller Owen, *In Camp and Battle with the Washington Artillery of New Orleans* (Louisiana: LSU Press, 1995), p. 128; Laura V. Hale & Stanley S. Philips, *History of the Forty-Ninth Virginia Infantry C.S.A.* (Virginia: published by the authors, 1981), p. 48.

14. Stuart, *SHSP*, p. 282.

15. Carl Schurz, Diary, August 31, 1862, Schurz Papers, Library of Congress. Schurz commanded the Third Division, First Corps, Army of Virginia; Joseph Willard, Diary, September 1, 1862, Willard Family Papers, Library of Congress. Willard was an aide-de-camp to General Irvin McDowell. His family founded the famed Willard Hotel in Washington, D.C.

16. Tolbert Report, *O.R.*, ser. 1, vol. 12, pt. 2, p. 538.

17. Pope, *O.R.*, ser. 1, vol. 12, pt. 2, p. 84; Hennessy, p. 445.

18. Ibid.

19. Pope, *O.R.,* ser. 1, vol. 12, pt. 3, p. 785.

20. Charles E. Davis, Jr., *Three Years in the Army* (Boston: Estes and Lauriat, 1894), p. 119; Austin C. Stearns, *Three Years with Company K* (Rutherford: Fairleigh Dickinson

University Press, 1976), p. 168; Peter Cozzens, *General John Pope: A Life for the Nation* (Urbana: University of Illinois Press, 2000), pp. 190–91.

21. David S. Sparks, editor, *Inside Lincoln's Army: The Diary of Marsena Rudolph Patrick, Provost Marshal General, Army of the Potomac* (New York: Thomas Yoseloff, 1964), p. 137; Carl A. Morrell, editor, *Seymour Dexter, Union Army: Journal and Letters of Civil War Service in Co. K, 23rd New York Volunteer Infantry* (Jefferson, N.C.: McFarland & Co., 1996), p. 81; McDowell Report, *O.R.*, ser. 1, vol. 12, pt. 2, p. 344.

22. Sparks, p. 137; William Gardiner, "Incidents of Cavalry Experiences During General Pope's Campaign" in *MOLLUS—Rhode Island,* vol. 34, pt. 3 (Wilmington, N.C.: Broadfoot Publishers, 1993), pp. 444–46.

23. This point is very near the modern intersection of State Road 50 and Jermantown Road. A modern westward view down State Road 50 towards Ox Hill from this intersection will still show how the ground slopes noticeably downward towards the Difficult Run streambed, thus giving an excellent defensive position to the Union defenders.

24. Theodore B. Gates, *The "Ulster Guard" [20th NY State Militia] and the War of the Rebellion* (New York: Benjamin Tyrell, 1879), pp. 282–85; Gates Report, *O.R.*, ser. 1, vol. 12, pt. 2, p. 377; Osborne, ed., *The Civil War Diaries of Theodore B. Gates* (Hightstown: Longstreet House, 1991), p. 37.

25. R. L. T. Beale, p. 36; J. J. Shoemaker, *Shoemaker's Battery, Stuart Horse Artillery, Pelham's Battalion* (Gaithersburg, Md.: Butternut & Blue, 1994), p. 21; Gates, pp. 282–85; Gates Report, *O.R.*, ser. 1, vol. 12, pt. 2, p. 377.

26. R. L. T. Beale, p. 36; Frederic Denison, *Sabres and Spurs: The First Regiment Rhode Island Cavalry* (R.I.: First Rhode Island Cavalry Veterans Association, 1876), pp. 148–49.

27. Stuart, *SHSP*, p. 282.

28. McDowell Report, *O.R.*, ser. 1, vol. 12, pt. 2, p. 344; Ricketts Report, *O.R.*, ser. 1, vol. 12, pt. 2, p. 385. The modern Jermantown Road extension that runs between Routes 50 and 29 did not exist during the Civil War, however this three-tenths of a mile stretch provides a good approximation of the Union defensive line at Germantown during the battle.

29. von Borcke, p. 169; Michael Palmer, *Lee Moves North: Robert E. Lee on the Offensive* (New York: John Wiley & Sons, 1998), pp. 12–14.

30. von Borcke, p. 171.

31. Stuart, *SHSP*, p. 282; Robert R. Smith, "The Battle Of Ox Hill" in *Fairfax County And The War Between The States* (Fairfax County Civil War Centennial Commission, Fairfax, Va., 1961), p. 41.

32. D'Anne Evans, *The Story of Oakton, Virginia: 1758–1982* (Oakton, Va.: Greater Oakton Citizens Association, 1982), pp. 41–42.

33. *O.R.,* ser. 1, vol. 12, pt. 3, p. 788.

Chapter 4

1. Ezra J. Warner, *Generals in Blue* (Baton Rouge: Louisiana State University Press, 1964), pp. 394–95; William F. McConnell, *Remember Reno: A Biography of Major General Jesse L. Reno* (Shippensburg, Pa.: White Mane Publishing, 1996), p. 59.

2. See appendix 1 for a brief biography of Isaac Stevens.

3. E. M. Woodward, *Our Campaigns: The Second Regiment Pennsylvania Reserve Volunteers* (Shippensburg: Burd Street Press, 1995), pp. 144–45; Hazard Stevens, *The Life of Isaac Ingalls Stevens, 2 Vols.* (Boston: Houghton, Mifflin & Co., 1900), Vol. 2, p. 478; *O.R.,* ser. 1, vol. 12, pt. 2, p. 395.

4. Photocopy of undated holograph manuscript by Hazard Stevens describing the battle of Chantilly, collection of the author; Stevens, *Life of Isaac Stevens,* p. 480.

5. Rice memoir, USAMHI, p. 62; William Todd, *The 79th New York Highlanders* (New York: Brandow, Barton and Co, 1886), p. 215. Todd served on General Stevens' staff and was an eyewitness to the attack; Stevens, p. 481.

6. Charles F. Walcott, "The Battle of Chantilly" in *Papers of the Military Historical Society of Massachusetts.* vol. 12, 1895, pp. 150–51; Samuel Bates, *A Brief History of the One Hundredth Regiment (Roundheads)* (New Castle, Pa.: J. C. Stevenson, 1884), p. 15.

7. *O.R.,* ser. 1, vol. 12, pt. 2, p. 85.

8. Rice memoir, USAMHI, p. 63. This is the only physical description of the cornfield's pre-battle condition known to the author.

9. Stevens, p. 484.

10. Walcott, p. 154.

11. Rice memoir, USAMHI, p. 63.

12. "A Roundhead Who Was with Pope's Army at Chantilly" in *Washington National Tribune*, April 13, 1899.

13. Sandy Barnard, editor, *Campaigning with the Irish Brigade: Pvt. John Ryan, 28th Massachusetts* (Terre Haute, Ind.: AST Press, 2001), pp. 57–58.

14. Todd, pp. 218–19.

15. Jackson Report, *O.R.,* ser. 1, vol. 12, pt. 2, p. 647.

16. Todd, p. 217.

17. James Huffman, *Ups and Downs of a Confederate Soldier* (New York: William Rudge's Sons, 1940), p. 62. Huffman was with the 10th Virginia infantry.

18. Samuel Benjamin, "We Cleared Their Way" in *Civil War Times Illustrated* 32, no. 1 (Mar./Apr. 1993): 116–17.

19. McClendon, pp. 123–24.

20. Stevens, pp. 484–85; Todd, p. 219.

21. William Thompson Lusk, *War Letters of William Thompson Lusk* (New York: Privately Printed, 1911), p. 180. Thompson was a captain in the 79th New York.

22. *National Tribune*, April 13, 1899.

23. Rice memoir, USAMHI, p. 63.

24. Andrew J. Morrison, Letter dated September 22, 1862, Manassas National Battlefield Park Library. Morrison served with the 100th Pennsylvania; William Gilfillan Gavin, *Campaigning with the Roundheads: A History of the 100th Pennsylvania Volunteer Infantry Regiment in the American Civil War 1861–1865* (Dayton: Morningside, 1989), p. 150.

25. See appendix 2 for a brief biography of Philip Kearny.

26. Samuel Heintzelman, Diary and Journal, Heintzelman Papers, Library of Congress; Heintzelman Report, *O.R.,* ser. 1, vol. 12, pt. 2, p. 414.

27. Todd, pp. 220–21.

28. Robinson Report, *O.R.,* ser. 1, vol. 12, pt. 2, p. 423; Poe report, *O.R.,* ser. 1, vol. 12, pt. 2, p. 436; Erasmus C. Gilbreath, Unpublished memoir of the 20th Indiana Infantry, Manassas National Battlefield Park Library. Gilbreath was a major with the 20th.

29. Robert Knox Sneden, Memoirs, Virginia Historical Society, vol. 3, pt. 4, August 30, 1862 to September 15, 1862, pp. 623–24.

30. Stevens, p. 485; Lusk, p. 180.

31. John Stevenson Memoir; Morrison Papers, The Civil War Library and Museum, Philadelphia, Pa. Stevenson served in the 100th Pennsylvania "Roundhead" regiment. In his memoir, Stevenson writes that he "had the distinction of carrying the last message ever sent by General Stevens."

32. Terry Johnston, editor, *"Him on One Side and Me on the Other": Civil War Letters of Alexander Campbell, 79th New York Infantry Regiment and James Campbell, 1st*

South Carolina Battalion (Columbia: University of South Carolina, 1999), p. 115; *National Tribune*, September 8, 1862; Todd, p. 220.

33. A close look at the preserved topography of the small Ox Hill Battlefield Park reveals how the final 100 yards of the charge from Stevens' men would have been up a very noticeable incline against Hays' Louisianans who were crouching behind a snake rail fence. This fence was only a few feet to the south of the site of the Kearney/Stevens monuments.

34. Horatio Belcher, Diary, William M. Fenton Papers, Bentley Historical Library, University of Michigan.

35. Stevens, pp. 485–86; Todd, p. 220. The exact spot of Stevens' death is considered to be at or very near to his memorial marker. See "The Battlefield Today."

36. Hazard Stevens, Family Papers, Library of Congress, Letter dated May 2, 1877, from Samuel Benjamin to Hazard Stevens.

37. Forno Report, *O.R.*, ser. 1, vol. 12, pt. 2, p. 718.

38. Early Report, *O.R.*, ser. 1, vol. 12, pt. 2, pp. 714–15.

39. James P. Gannon, *Irish Rebels, Confederate Tigers: A History of the 6th Louisiana Volunteers, 1861–1865* (Campbell, Calif.: Savas, 1998), p. 120.

40. William C. Oates, *The War Between the Union and the Confederacy and its Lost Opportunities with a History of the 15th Alabama Regiment* (New York: Neale, 1905), p. 150.

41. Gregory C. White, *This Most Bloody and Cruel Drama: A History of the 31st Georgia Infantry* (Baltimore, Md.: Butternut and Blue, 1997), p. 45.

42. William B. Colston, Civil War Recollections, Frederica Trapnell Papers, Virginia Historical Society, p. 18.

43. James Cooper Nisbett, *Four Years on the Firing Line* (Chattanooga, Tenn.: Imperial Press, 1914), pp. 146–47; Jubal A. Early, *Narrative of the War Between the States* (Philadelphia: Lippincott, 1912), p. 99; Henry W. Thomas, *History of the Doles-Cook Brigade* (Dayton, Ohio: Morningside, 1981), pp. 1, 237.

44. Oates, p. 150; Thomas, p. 221.

45. Early, *O.R.*, pp. 714–15; Jubal A. Early, *Narrative of the War Between the States* (Philadelphia: Lippincott, 1912), pp. 129–30; Charles Osborne, *Jubal: The Life and Times of General Jubal A. Early, CSA* (Chapel Hill, N.C.: Algonquin Books of Chapel Hill, 1992) pp. 113–14.

46. Richard L. Armstrong, *25th Virginia Infantry and 9th Battalion Virginia Infantry* (Lynchburg, Va.: H. E. Howard), 1990, p. 46.

47. *Letters of the Civil War* "Letter of Pvt. Dennis Ford, 28th Massachusetts, Co. H, 6 September 1862." available at http://www.28thmass.org/Letters/Letters .htm#anchor118820—World Wide Web.

48. Early Report, *O.R.*, ser. 1, vol. 12, pt. 2, pp. 714–15.

49. Charles R. Adams, editor, *A Post of Honor: The Pryor Letters, 1861–63* (Fort Valley, Ga.: Garret Publications, 1989), p. 252.

50. Hewitt, " A Confederate Foreign Legion," pp. 64–65.

51. *New York Tribune*, September 3, 1862.

52. Oliver C. Bosbyshell, *The 48th in the War* (Philadelphia: Avil Printing Co., 1895), p. 70; Elisha Hunt Rhodes, *All for the Union: Civil War Diary and Letters of Elisha Hunt Rhodes, 2nd Rhode Island* (New York: Orion, 1985), p. 79. It is asserted by the author with the highest confidence that a statement on the severity of the weather was the common thread running through virtually *every* soldier's account or reminiscence of this battle.

53. James Longstreet, *From Manassas to Appomattox: Memoirs of the Civil War In America* (Philadelphia: Lippincott, 1896), p. 193; L. Van Loan Naisawald, "A Nasty Little Battle in the Rain" in *Civil War Times Illustrated* 3, no. 3 (June 1964): 15.

54. Margaret Leech, *Reveille In Washington* (New York: Carroll and Graf, 1991), p. 193.

55. Photocopy of undated holograph manuscript by Hazard Stevens describing the battle of Chantilly, collection of the author.

56. Lewis Nunnelee, Diary, September 1, 1862, Eleanor Brockenbrough Library, Museum of the Confederacy, Richmond, Va. Nunnelee served with the Stuart Horse Artillery.

57. Pender Report, *O.R.*, ser. 1, vol. 12, pt. 2, p. 698.

58. Edwards Report, *O.R.*, ser. 1, vol. 16, p. 696; J. F. J. Caldwell, *The History of a Brigade of South Carolinians, Known First as Gregg's and Subsequently as McGowan's Brigade* (Dayton, Ohio: Morningside, 1974), pp. 67–68.

59. Thomas Report, *O.R.*, ser. 1, vol. 12, pt. 2, p. 703.

60. Archer Report, *O.R.*, ser. 1, vol. 12, pt. 2, p. 702.

61. Col. S. Crutchfield Report, *O.R.*, ser. 1, vol. 12, pt. 2, p. 654; Charles F. Walcott, "A Revisit to the Fields of Manassas and Chantilly" in *Papers of the Military Historical Society of Massachusetts*. vol. 2 (Boston: Military Historical Society of Massachusetts, 1895), pp. 189–90.

62. Andrew L. Fowler, *Memoirs of the Late Adjt. Andrew L. Fowler of the 51st N. Y. V.* (New York: Ferris and Pratt, 1863), p. 57; Walcott, *Battle of Chantilly...*, p. 156.

63. Jerome M. Loving, editor, *Civil War Letters of George Washington Whitman* (Durham: Duke University Press, 1975), p. 63; Fowler, p. 57.

64. Henry W. Francis, Letter to his wife, September 4, 1862, Henry W. Francis Letters, Records of the 51st Regiment A0087, New York State Archives.

65. James Madison Stone, *Personal Recollections of the Civil War* (Boston: Self-Published, 1918), p. 72.

66. George C. Parker, "I feel...just like writing you a letter..." in *Civil War Times* 16, no. 1 (April 1977): 15. Letter to his mother-in-law dated October 15, 1862.

67. Charles F. Walcott, *History of the Twenty-First Regiment Massachusetts Volunteers* (Boston: Houghton Mifflin, 1882), pp. 162–63; Stone, p. 73.

68. Robert R. Smith, "The Battle Of Ox Hill" in *Fairfax County and the War Between the States,* Fairfax County Civil War Centennial Commission, Fairfax, Va., 1961, p. 52.

69. Lucie F. Hanson, Letter regarding death of Augustus Upton, 21st Mass., 1862. Connecticut Historical Society; Letter to the Editor, *Roxbury City Gazette*, September 11, 1862.

70. *The 15 Most Underrated Battles of the Civil War.* Civil War Interactive, 5 Dec 2001, available at http://205.247.235.71/urbattle15.htm—World Wide Web.

71. John Schillich, Diary, September 1, 1862, Historical Society of Montgomery County, Pa; Charles A. Cuffel, *Durell's Battery in the Civil War* (Philadelphia: Craig, Finley & Co., 1900), pp. 68–69; Todd, p. 221.

72. Sauers, ed., p. 77.

73. Annette Tapert, editor, *The Brothers' War: Civil War Letters to Their Loved Ones from the Blue and the Gray* (New York: Times Books, 1988), p. 85. Letter dated September 5, 1862, from Capt. Henry Pearson, 6th New Hampshire regiment, to a friend back home.

74. Lyman Jackman, *History of the Sixth New Hampshire Regiment* (Concord: Republican Press Association, 1891), p. 88.

75. Samuel Beddal, Diary, U.S. Military History Institute, Carlisle, Pa.; John Michael Priest, *From New Bern to Fredericksburg: Captain James Wren's Diary* (Shippensburg, Pa.: White Mane Publishing, 1990), p. 59; Tapert, ed., p. 85.

76. Hosea Towne, Letter dated September 6, 1862, New Hampshire Historical Society, Concord, N.H; Upton Letter, September 3, 1862.

77. Harry E. Ford, *History of the 101st Regiment* (Syracuse: Times Publishing Co., 1898), p. 39. This title references the 101st New York Infantry.

78. Peter P. Dalton, *With Our Faces to the Foe: A History of the 4th Maine Infantry in the War of the Rebellion* (Union, Maine: Union Publishing Co., 1998), p. 185.

79. Stephen W. Sears, editor, *On Campaign with the Army of the Potomac: The Civil War Journal of Theodore Ayrault Dodge* (New York: Cooper Square Press, 2001), p. 91.

80. Birney Report, *O.R.*, ser. 1, vol. 12, pt. 2, p. 418; Thomas C. H. Smith, Manuscript, "The Battle of Chantilly," transcribed by Joseph C. Leasure, Virginia Room, Fairfax County Public Library, p. 15. Smith was a staff officer of Pope's, and therefore not an eyewitness to the battle. His manuscript was based on the *O.R.* and eyewitness accounts relayed to him after the battle which includes the material quoted here. Henry Foster diary transcript. Foster was a captain in the 40th New York.

81. William Styple, editor, *Writing and Fighting the Civil War: Soldier Correspondence to the New York Sunday Mercury* (Kearny, N.J.: Belle Grove Publishing, 2000), p. 132.

82. James Martin, et al., *History of the 57th Regiment, Pennsylvania Veteran Volunteer Infantry* (Kearny, N.J.: Belle Grove Publishing, 1985), pp. 56–57.

83. Randolph Report, *O.R.*, ser. 1, vol. 12, pt. 2, p. 420.

84. Pender Report, *O.R.*, ser. 1, vol. 12, pt. 2, p. 698.

85. James Lane, "History of Lane's North Carolina Brigade" in *SHSP*, vol. 8, no. 4, p. 154.

86. Sneden, Memoirs, Virginia Historical Society. vol. 3, pt. 4. August 30, 1862 to September 15, 1862, pp. 631–32.

87. Ibid.

88. Janet B. Hewet, editor, *Supplement to the Official Records of the Union and Confederate Armies,* serial 37, vol. 25, pt. 2 (Wilmington, N.C.: Broadfoot Publishing Co., 1996), p. 209; Dalton, p. 185; Walcott. "The Battle of Chantilly," p. 155.

89. "Extract From A Private Letter," *New York Times*, September 13, 1862. Though printed without the name of its author, this letter was probably from the pen of Kearny's aide de camp, then-Lieutenant Charles Graves, as its context and style is almost identical to Graves' letter found in *From the Peninsula.*

90. Warner, *Generals in Blue*, p. 34.

91. Lusk, pp. 180–81.

92. Reverend Robert A. Brown, Letter to his wife, September 5, 1862, Tami McConahy Collection, World Wide Web @ http://members.aol.com/dwelchk2/browne64.html

93. Parker, p. 15.

94. Walcott, p. 157; Stone, p. 74.

95. Todd, p. 221; Walcott, *History of the 21st...*, p. 164.

96. Walcott, pp. 158–60; Walcott, *History of the 21st ...*, p. 165.

97. William B. Styple, *Letters from the Peninsula: The Civil War Letters of General Philip Kearny* (Kearny, N.J.: Belle Grove Publishing Company, 1988), p. 173; Frederick C. Floyd, *History of the Fortieth (Mozart) Regiment* (Boston: F. H. Gilson Co., 1909), p. 178.

98. John Watts de Peyster, *Personal and Military History of Philip Kearny* (New York: Rice & Gage, 1869), pp. 462–63.

99. United Daughters of the Confederacy, *Confederate Reminiscences and Letters 1861–1865, Volume I* (Ga.: self-published, 1995), p. 11; W. S. Nye, "Kearny's Death Grieved Both Sides" in *Civil War Times* 2 (January 1961): 24.

100. Various contributors, "Who Killed General Philip Kearny?" in *Confederate Veteran* (June 1907). Others claiming credit have included members of the 9th Louisiana (*Confederate Veteran*, November, 1906); Joseph W. A. Whitehorne, "A Beastly, Comfortless Conflict: The Battle Of Chantilly" in *Blue & Gray* 4, no. 5 (May 1987): 53.

101. Victor Thacker, editor, *French Harding: Civil War Memoirs* (Parsons, W.Va.: McClain Printing Co., 2000), p. 73.

102. Stephen W. Sears, editor, *For Country, Cause and Leader: The Civil War Journal of Charles B. Hayden* (New York: Ticknor & Fields, 1993), p. 282.

103. William Gardiner, Letter dated September 6, 1862, Ralph Brown Draughton Library, Auburn University.

104. Stone, p. 78; *O.R.* , ser. 1, vol. 12, pt. 2, p. 414.

105. Carol Drake Friedman, "Where Did the Hero's Body Lie" in *The Historical Society of Fairfax County, Virginia Yearbook, Vol. 24, 1993–1994.* (Fairfax: Historical Society of Fairfax, 1993), pp. 91–105. The author presents numerous pieces of circumstantial, yet convincing evidence in this article to assert that Kearny's body was taken by the Confederates to the plantation home of Charles Stuart, known as "Chantilly," rather than the more modest farm home of one Charles Stewart, not the same and unrelated, that was closer to the battlefield; Hunter, p. 506; Thomas Kearny, *General Philip Kearny: Battle Soldier of Five Wars* (New York: G. P. Putnam's Sons, 1937), p. 388.

106. Johnson and Buel, eds. *Battles and Leaders of the Civil War, 4 Vols.,* vol. 2, pt. 2 (Harrisburg: The Archive Society, 1991), p. 538.

107. T. Kearny, p. 388; Styple, *Letters from the Peninsula,* pp. 194–97.

108. South Carolina Division: United Daughters of the Confederacy, *Recollections and Reminiscences 1861–1865, Volume I* (S.C.: self published, 1990), p. 204.

109. G. W. Beale, *A Lieutenant of Cavalry in Lee's Army* (Boston: The Gorsham Press, 1918), p. 42; Walter H. Taylor, *General Lee: His Campaigns in Virginia, 1861–1865, With Personal Reminiscences* (Dayton, Ohio: Morningside, 1975), p. 116.

110. South Carolina UDC, *Recollections...,* p. 204; Joseph D. Baker, Papers. U.S. Military History Institute. Carlisle, Pa.. Letter to his mother dated September 30, 1862; James Martin, *History of the 57th...,* p. 57.

111. *Washington Star,* September 3, 1862.

112. Walcott, p. 160; Parker, p. 16.

113. Stone, p. 74.

114. Walcott, *History of the 21st Mass...,* p. 166.

115. Clark Report, *O.R.,* ser. 1, vol. 9, p. 24.

116. McConnell, p. 68.

117. Parker, p. 16.

118. Ibid.

119. Reminiscence of Dr. Hunter Maguire, Stonewall Jackson's Chief Surgeon, *SHSP,* vol. 19, p. 311.

120. Ford, p. 39.

121. T. Harry Williams, "The Reluctant Warrior: The Diary of N. K. Nichols" in *Civil War History,* vol. 3, no. 1, Iowa: State University of Iowa (March 1957): 36. Norman K. Nichols served in the 101st New York. Like many, his true talents lay in avoiding battle, as his diary illustrates.

122. Dodge, p. 90.

123. Birney Report, *O.R.,* ser. 1, vol. 12, pt. 2, p. 418; Poe Report, *O.R.,* ser. 1, vol. 12, pt. 2, p. 436.

124. Sears, *For Country Cause...,* p. 282.

125. Osmun Latrobe, Diary, p. 8, Virginia Historical Society. Latrobe served with General D. R. Jones in Longstreet's division; W. H. Andrews, *Footprints of a Regiment: A Recollection of the 1st Georgia Regulars 1861–1865* (Atlanta: Longstreet Press, 1992), pp. 69–70.

126. W. H. Andrews, "Tige Anderson's Brigade At Ox Hill" in *Atlanta Journal,* June 22, 1901.

127. Glenn C. Oldaker, compiler, *Centennial Tales: Memoirs of Colonel Chester S. Bassett French* (New York: Carlton Press, 1962), p. 45. French was an extra aide-de-camp to Generals Lee and Jackson.

128. D. Jones Report, *O.R.*, ser. 1, vol. 12, pt. 2, p. 580; Taylor, pp. 116–17.

129. James Longstreet, "Our March Against Pope" in *The Century Magazine* 31, no. 4, New York: The Century Co. (February 1886): 610; Longstreet, *From Manassas...*, p. 194.

Chapter 5

1. Pyne, pp. 86–87.

2. Wise, *Campaigns...*, p. 162; Wilbur Dickerson, Letter to the *National Tribune*, December 8, 1904. Dickerson was a drummer boy with the 8th Michigan.

3. Parker, pp. 220–21.

4. Todd, p. 224.

5. Kent Richards, *Isaac I. Stevens: Young Man in a Hurry* (Pullman, Wash.: Washington State University Press, 1993), pp. 389–90.

6. Terry Jones, *Lee's Tigers: The Louisiana Infantry in the Army of Northern Virginia* (Baton Rouge: Louisiana State University, 1987), p. 126. Originally, letter from William Behan to his father, October 14, 1862, in Behan Family Papers, Tulane University.

7. Wayland Fuller Dunaway, *Reminiscences of a Rebel* (New York: Neale, 1913), pp. 45–47. Dunaway was the former captain of Company I, 40th Virginia Regiment.

8. Lane, *SHSP*, vol. 8, no. 4, p. 154; Armstrong, p. 46.

9. Benjamin L. Farinholt, Diary, September 1, 1862. Virginia Historical Society, Richmond, Va.

10. Todd, p. 223; Wise, p. 106.

11. Cuffel, p. 69.

12. Ford, p. 39; Parker, p. 221.

13. Todd, p. 224; Schiller Diary, September 2, 1862.

14. Poe Report, p. 436; Robinson Report, p. 423; Sauers, ed., p. 77.

15. D. G. Crotty, *Four Years Campaigning in the Army of the Potomac* (Grand Rapids, Mich.: Dygert Brothers, 1874), pp. 64–65.

16. Charles F. Morse, "From Second Bull Run to Antietam" in *MOLLUS—Missouri,* vol. 14, no. 1 (Chapel Hill, N.C.: Broadfoot,) pp. 270–77.

17. James P. Gannon, *Irish Rebels, Confederate Tigers: History of the 6th Louisiana Volunteers, 1861–1865* (Campbell, Calif.: Savas, 1998), p. 120.

Chapter 6

1. Kyd Douglas, p. 144.

2. One of two such houses on the battlefield was the Milan house, later known to Fairfax historians as "Oakley." Though no longer in existence, the house was for over a century a prominent fixture at the southern end of the field, well within the Union lines of attack and just south of Federal batteries. The house ultimately came into the ownership of Fairfax County and was intentionally burned to the ground as part of a firefighters' training exercise in the 1980s. Numerous Union soldiers, while in the "hospital" there, had left their names and messages scribbled on the plaster walls. Relatives of these men would travel to the site for years afterward to seek their writings. Dozens of Union soldiers who died during Ox Hill were rumored to have been buried on the grounds but their remains were ultimately moved after the war. Source—Imlay, John et al. *The Oakley Site 44FX734.* Archeological Society of Virginia, Northern Va. Chapter. Occasional Paper 86–2, Nov. 1986.

3. Morrison Letter dated September 22, 1862.

4. W. R. and M. B Houghton, *Two Boys in the Civil War and After* (Montgomery, Ala.: The Paragon Press, 1912), p. 27.

5. Spencer Glasgow Welch, *A Confederate Surgeon's Letters to His Wife* (Marietta, Ga.: Continental Book Co., 1954), pp. 28–30.

6. Alfred Bellard, *Gone for a Soldier: The Civil War Memoirs of Private Alfred Bellard* (Boston: Little, Brown & Co., 1975), pp. 145–46.

7. Bellard, p. 146.

8. Clara Barton, Diary, August 30, 1862, Library of Congress.

9. Clara Barton, Papers, Letter to Lizzie Shaver, September 4, 1862, Library of Congress; William E. Barton, *The Life of Clara Barton* (Boston: Houghton Mifflin Co., 1922), p. 185.

10. Hardtack was a standard army food item consisting of flour and water, which was then formed and baked into square crackers. It was so hard it sometimes cracked teeth.

11. Barton Papers, LOC; Stephen Oates, *Clara Barton: A Woman of Valor* (New York: The Free Press, 1994), pp. 73–74; Elizabeth Brown Pryor, "Clara Barton at Fairfax Station" in *Northern Virginia Heritage* 3, no. 2 (June 1981): 3–8.

12. Herman Haupt, *Reminiscences of General Herman Haupt* (Milwaukee, Wis.: Wright & Joys, 1901), pp. 133–34.

13. Beale, pp. 67–68.

14. N. Netherton, R. Rose, D. Meyer, P. Wagner, M. DiVincenzo, *Fairfax, Virginia: A City Traveling through Time* (Fairfax: History of Fairfax Round Table, 1997), pp. 26–27; Pryor, pp. 3–8.

15. Rufus R. Dawes, *Service with the Sixth Wisconsin Volunteers* (Dayton, Ohio: Morningside, 1984), p. 75.

16. Gerrish, p. 25.

17. Jackman, p. 93.

18. Calvin Cutter, Unpublished Memoir, Library of Congress, p. 39.

19. Cecil Eby, Jr., editor, *A Virginia Yankee in the Civil War: The Diaries of David Hunter Strother* (Chapel Hill, N.C.: University of North Carolina, 1961), p. 100.

20. Peter R. Henriques, "Second Manassas and the End of the War For Corporal James Tanner, USA" in *Northern Virginia Heritage* 6 no. 2, Fairfax, Va. (1984): 6.

21. Haupt Reports, *O.R.*, ser. 1, vol. 12, pt. 3, pp. 775–76; William Quentin Maxwell, *Lincoln's Fifth Wheel: The Political History of the United States Sanitary Commission* (New York: Longmans, Green and Co., 1956), p. 166; Francis A. Lord, *Lincoln's Railroad Man: Herman Haupt* (Rutherford: Fairleigh Dickinson University Press, 1969), pp. 136–37.

22. Reno Letter, *O.R.*, ser. 1, vol. 51, pt. 1, p. 782.

23. Sanitary Commission Letter, *New York Times*, September 12, 1862.

24. Edwin Palmer, *The Second Brigade, or Camp Life by a Volunteer* (Montpelier, Vt.: self-published, 1864), p. 87.

25. Netherton, Rose, et al., p. 28.

26. John Magruder, Letter to his Father, December 4, 1862, Magruder Family Letters, Library of Virginia, Richmond, Va.

27. Ibid.; Sneden Memoir, vol. 3, pt. 4, p. 606.

28. Netherton, Rose, et al., p. 27. William McKnight's letter here was dated December 12, 1862. The spelling and grammar have been maintained from the original letter.

29. *Alexandria (Virginia) Gazette*, August 29, 1862.

30. Gamble, p. 105.

31. Eugenia B. Smith, *Centreville, Virginia: Its History and Architecture* (Fairfax: Fairfax County Office of Planning, 1973), p. 59. Originally taken from the *Washington Sunday Star*, quoting from an account of the dedication of monuments on the Bull Run battlefield, June 11, 1865.

Chapter 7

1. Belcher, Diary.
2. William Dorsey Pender, *One of Lee's Best Men: The Civil War Letters of General William Dorsey Pender* (Chapel Hill, N.C.: University of North Carolina, 1995), p. 170.
3. E. Porter Alexander, *Military Memoirs of a Confederate* (New York: Da Capo Press, 1993), p. 217.
4. A. Hunter, *SHSP*, vol. 10, nos. 10–11. Richmond, 1884, pp. 506–7.
5. Wise, p. 163; M. Shuler Diary, September 2, 1862; Abner Hopkins Diary, Virginia Historical Society. Hopkins was the chaplain of the 2nd Virginia Infantry; Diary of Buckner Randolph, Virginia Historical Society. Randolph was with the 49th Virginia Infantry; Lee, p. 586.
6. Bellard, p. 146.
7. Priest, *Wren Diary*, pp. 59–60.
8. Samuel Elias Mays, "Famous Battles as a Confederate Private Saw Them" in *Tyler's Quarterly Historical and Genealogical Magazine* 4, no. 4, Richmond (April 1923): 399; Stuart Report, *SHSP*, p. 282.
9. Mays, p. 399.
10. Manley Wade Wellman, *Giant in Gray: A Biography of Wade Hampton* (New York: Charles Scribners Sons, 1949), p. 89.
11. James A. Wright, *No More Gallant a Deed: A Civil War Memoir of the First Minnesota Volunteers* (St. Paul: Minnesota Historical Society Press, 2001), p. 187.
12. Ibid., pp. 187–88.
13. Ernest Linden Waitt, compiler, *History of the 19th Regiment, Massachusetts Volunteer Infantry* (Salem, Mass.: The Salem Press, 1906), p. 122.
14. John Reynolds, Unpublished reminiscences of service with the 19th Massachusetts regiment, 1861–1862, Massachusetts Historical Society, pp. 111–12; Waitt, compiler, *History of the 19th Regiment*, p. 123.
15. Henry W. Moore, *"Chained to Virginia While Carolina Bleeds": Civil War Correspondence of H. W. Moore and J. W. Moore* (Walterboro, S.C.: Self-published, 1996), p. 128; Hampton Report, *O.R.*, ser. 1, vol. 19, pt. 1, p. 822; Stuart Report, *SHSP*; von Borcke, pp. 173–75; Waitt, *History of the 19th Regiment*, p. 123.
16. Richard Moe, *The Last, Full Measure: The Life and Death of the First Minnesota Volunteers* (New York: Henry Holt & Co., 1993), p. 174; John G. B. Adams, *Reminiscences of the 19th Massachusetts Regiment* (Boston: Wright Potter, 1899), pp. 42–43.
17. Reynolds, Unpublished reminiscences, pp. 111–12.
18. Near the intersection of modern Route 123 and Germantown Rd.
19. William Lochren, "Narrative of the First Regiment" in *Minnesota in the Civil and Indian Wars, 1861–1865,* vol. 1 (St. Paul, Minn.: Pioneer Press, 1891), pp. 24–25.
20. James W. Groat, *Pages Clothed in the Plainest of Dress: The Groat Diary* (Anoka, Minn.: Anoka County Historical Society, 1988), p. 27.
21. Adele H. Mitchell, editor, *The Letters of Major General James E. B. Stuart* (Richmond: Stuart-Mosby Historical Society, 1990), p. 263.
22. Groat, p. 27.
23. Waitt, compiler, *History of the 19th Regiment*, p. 124; Wright, p. 190.
24. Moe, pp. 175–76; Reynolds Reminiscences, pp. 111–12; Adams, John G. B., pp. 42–43.
25. Stuart Report, *SHSP;* Denison, p. 149.
26. Hotchkiss, p. 78.
27. Jedediah Hotchkiss, Letter to his wife, September 8, 1862, Hotchkiss Family Papers, Library of Congress; Mitchell, *Stuart Letters*, p. 263.

28. Lee Report, *O.R.*, ser. 1, vol. 12, pt. 2, p. 558.

29. Hotchkiss, *Make Me A Map...*, p. 78.

30. *New York Tribune,* September 4, 1862; Hunter, *SHSP*, p. 507.

31. Lawrence Cavanaugh, editor, "The Diary of Isaac R. Rathbun" in *New York History* 36, New York State Historical Association (July 1955): 340.

32. Haynes, pp. 14–15; Hotchkiss, Jedediah, Holograph copy of diary, September 2, 1862, Library of Congress.

33. Eisenschiml, p. 242.

34. Freeman & McWhiney, eds., *Lee's Dispatches*, p. 62.

35. Lee to Davis, *O.R.*, ser. 1, vol. 19, pt. 2, pp. 591–92.

36. John Winsmith, Letter dated September 3, 1862, Eleanor S. Brockenbrough Library, Museum of the Confederacy, Richmond, Va.; Boulware Diary, p. 20.

37. Jed. Hotchkiss, "Virginia" in *Confederate Military History, 12 Vols.*, vol. 3 (Atlanta: Confederate Publishing Co., 1898), p. 335.

38. Point of Rocks is the point where modern Route 15 crosses the Potomac River.

39. Edwin Baker Loving, Reminiscences, Personal Papers Collection, Library of Richmond, Richmond, Va., p. 33; John Magruder Letters, December 4, 1862.

40. John W. Stepp and William I. Hill, editors, *Mirror of War: The Washington Star Reports the Civil War* (Englewood, N.J.: Prentice Hall, 1961), pp. 147–48.

41. George McClellan, *McClellan's Own Story* (New York: Charles Webster & Co., 1887), pp. 532–33.

42. B. Franklin Cooling, *Symbol, Sword & Shield: Defending Washington During the Civil War* (Hamden: Archon Books, 1975), p. 133; McClellan, pp. 535–36.

43. Lewis Crater, *History of the Fiftieth Regiment, Pennsylvania Veteran Volunteers, 1861–1865* (Reading, Pa.: Coleman Printing House, 1884), p. 30.

44. Bellard. p. 147.

45. Robert Garth Scott, editor, *Fallen Leaves: Civil War Letters of Major Henry Livermore Abbott, 20th Massachusetts Infantry* (Kent, Ohio: Kent State University Press, 1991), p. 139.

46. Pope wire, *O.R.*, ser. 1, vol. 12, pt. 3, pp. 796–97.

47. Halleck wire, *O.R.*, ser. 1, vol. 12, pt. 3, p. 797.

48. McClellan, p. 537.

49. Wallace J. Schutz and Walter N. Trenerry, *Abandoned by Lincoln: A Military Biography of John Pope* (Chicago: University of Illinois Press, 1990), p. 151. (original –Cox, Jacob D. *Military Reminiscences of the Civil War*, 2 Vols. New York, 1900, vol. 1, pp. 244–45. General Hatch had received a strong rebuke from Pope several months earlier, which he felt unwarranted. His revenge was had with his taunt to Pope; McClellan, p. 537.

50. Jeffry Wert, *A Brotherhood of Valor* (New York: Simon & Schuster, 1999), p. 161.

51. Horace Greeley was the influential founding editor of the *New York Tribune*.

52. John H. B. Jenkins, Letter dated September 7, 1862 to Mary A. Benjamin, Alderman Library, University of Virginia.

53. Orlando M. Poe, Letter dated September 4, 1862, Orlando M. Poe Papers, Library of Congress.

54. *New York World*, September 6, 1862.

55. Pope's chief reason for requesting dismissal was so he could prefer charges and a subsequent court-martial against Army of the Potomac subordinates, chief among them Fitz-John Porter, stemming from Pope's certainty that they intentionally failed to carry out his orders during the battle of Second Manassas; *O.R.*, ser. 1, vol. 12, pt. 3, p. 817.

56. Stephen Sears, editor, *The Civil War Papers of George McClellan: Selected Correspondence 1860–1865* (New York: Ticknor & Fields, 1989), p. 403. Sears commentary.
57. Michael Burlingame & John Ettlinger, editors, *Inside Lincoln's White House: The Complete Civil War Diary of John Hay* (Carbondale: Southern Illinois University Press, 1997), p. 37.
58. Sears, editor, *Civil War Papers*, pp. 388–89.
59. Burlingame & Ettlinger, pp. 38–39.
60. John Whiteside, Letter dated October 16, 1862, Bentley Historical Library, University of Michigan.
61. *O.R.,* ser. 1, vol. 11, pt. 1, p. 103.
62. Sears, *Civil War Papers*, pp. 435–38.

Epilogue

1. G.A.R. stood for "Grand Army of the Republic," which was the organized veteran's group for Union soldiers in the decades following the war.
2. "Tribute To A Foe's Bravery" in *Confederate Veteran* 23, no. 12 (December 1915): 571; Richard L. Thompson, "Captain John Newton Ballard" in *The Historical Society of Fairfax County, Virginia Yearbook, Vol. 21, 1986–1988* (Fairfax: Historical Society of Fairfax, 1988), p. 100. A well-written piece on the Ballard's post-war ownership of the Reid Farm and how he came to donate it.
3. Georgie Boge and Margie Holder, *Paving over the Past* (Washington D.C.: Island Press, 1993), p. 68.
4. *Norfolk Virginian-Pilot*, October 13, 1986.

Appendix 3

1. Oliver Davis, *Life of David Bell Birney, Major General, United States Volunteers* (Philadelphia: King & Baird, 1867), pp. 74–75; Styple, *Letters from the Peninsula,* pp. 215–26.

Appendix 4

1. *Official Records*, ser. 1, vol. 12, pt.. 2, pp. 548–51; Sibley, F. Ray, Jr. *The Confederate Order of Battle, Volume 1: The Army of Northern Virginia* (Shippensburg, Pa.: White Mane, 1996); John Codman Ropes, "The Army Under Pope" in *Campaigns of the Civil War,* vol. 4, New York: Charles Scribners Sons, 1882; John J. Hennessy, *Return to Bull Run: The Campaign and Battle of Second Manassas* (New York: Simon and Schuster, 1993) pp. 551–67.
2. General Reno would be killed in action two weeks later at the September 14th battle of South Mountain.
3. Colonel Leasure was wounded at Second Manassas and not with his brigade at Ox Hill.
4. Colonel Farnsworth was severely wounded at Second Manassas and not present at the battle of Ox Hill.
5. Confederate Brigadier General William Starke would be killed in action two and a half weeks later at the battle of Antietam.
6. The commanding officer of the Stonewall Brigade at Second Manassas was Colonel William Baylor. He was killed in action during that battle. Major H. J. Williams of the 5th Virginia submitted the official report for the brigade regarding Ox Hill, "in the absence of more competent officers," and reports that Colonel A. J. Grigsby was commanding. (*O.R.,* ser. 1, vol. 19, pt. 1, p. 1010.)
7. Alexander G. Taliaferro was the uncle of Brigadier General William B. Taliaferro, who was wounded at Second Manassas.

8. General Branch would be killed in action two and a half weeks later at the battle of Antietam.

9. General Gregg would be killed December 15, 1862, at Fredericksburg. The official report of the Second Manassas campaign would be written by the then-commanding general, Samuel McGowan, who, due to injuries from Second Manassas, was not present at Ox Hill.

10. General Lawton would be severely wounded at the battle of Antietam two and a half weeks later.

11. Colonel Douglass would be killed in action at the battle of Antietam on September 17, 1862.

12. Colonel Strong would be killed in action two and a half weeks later at the battle of Antietam.

13. Hampton's brigade arrived into the Confederate camp after the Sept. 1 battle at Ox Hill had ended, but were engaged with the retreating Federal rear guard Sept. 2 at Fairfax and Flint Hill.

BIBLIOGRAPHY

Unpublished Manuscripts

Auburn University, Draughton Library
    Gardiner, William. Papers.
The Civil War Library and Museum, Philadelphia, Pa.
    Stevenson, John. Memoir; Morrison Papers.
Connecticut Historical Society
    Hanson, Lucie F. Letters, 1862.
Eastern Washington University
    Clark, Henry E. Memoir.
Fairfax County Public Library, Virginia Room, Fairfax, Va.
    Mauro, Charles V. Typescript, "The Battle of Chantilly."
    Smith, Thomas C. H. Manuscript, "The Battle of Chantilly."
 Library of Congress
    Barton, Clara. Papers.
    Cutter, Calvin, Dr. Memoir.
    Heintzelman, Samuel. Papers.
    Hotchkiss, Jedediah. Family Papers.
    Poe, Orlando M. Papers.
    Schurz, Carl. Diary.
    Shuler, M. Diary.
    Stevens, Hazard. Family Papers.
    Willard, Joseph, Major. Family Papers.
Manassas National Battlefield Park Library, Manassas, Va.
    Cross, Fred W. Manuscript, "The Battle of Chantilly Or Ox Hill,
        Sept. 1, 1862"

Gilbreath, Erasmus C. Memoir.

Hagood, James R. Memoirs.

Harper, W. P. Diary.

Morrison, Andrew J. Letters.

Massachusetts Historical Society, Boston, Mass.

Reynolds, John. "Reminiscences of service with the 19th Massachusetts, 1861–1862."

Historical Society of Montgomery County, Pa.

Schillich, John. Diary.

University of Michigan, Bentley Historical Library, Ann Arbor, Mich.

Belcher, Horatio. Diary, William M. Fenton Papers.

Noah, Elmer. Diary, Noah Family Papers.

Whiteside, John. Papers.

Museum of the Confederacy, Eleanor S. Brockenbrough Library, Richmond, Va.

Nunnelee, Lewis. Diary.

Winsmith, John. Papers.

New Hampshire Historical Society, Concord, N.H.

Upton, George E. Letters.

Towne, Hosea. Letters.

New York State Archives

Francis, Henry W. Letters.

Paul Taylor Collection.

Foster, Henry. Diary.

Stevens, Hazard. Papers.

University of Virginia, Alderman Library, Charlottesville, Va.

Jenkins, John H. B. Letters.

Virginia Historical Society, Richmond, Va.

Bolton, William H., Family Papers.

Colston, William B. Civil War Recollections, Frederica Trapnell Papers.

Farinholt, Benjamin L. Diary.

Hopkins, Abner Crump. Diary.

Latrobe, Osmun. Diary.

Randolph, Buckner Magill. Randolph Family Papers. Diary.

Sneden, Robert Knox. Memoirs.

Virginia Military Institute Archives.

Gatewood, Andrew C. L. Papers.

Library of Virginia, Richmond, Va.

Boulware, James Richmond. Diary.

Loving, Edwin Baker. Reminiscences.

Magruder Family Letters

Orr, James Wesley. Recollections, Personal Papers Collection.

United States Army Military History Institute, Carlisle, Pa.

Baker, Joseph D. Papers.

Beddal, Samuel. Diary.

Bracken, Elisha. Diary.

Rice, Nicholas. Memoir.

Bill Worsham Collection, Fairfax, Va.

Thompson, Wilfred W. Manuscript, "Campaigns of the 62nd & 155th Pennsylvania Regiments 1861–1865"

Government Documents

United States War Department. *The War of the Rebellion: A Compilation of the Official Records of the Union and Confederate Armies.* 128 volumes. Washington D.C., 1881–1902.

United States War Department. *Atlas to Accompany the Official Records of the Union and Confederate Armies.* 2 Vols. Washington D.C., 1891–1895.

Newspapers

Alexandria (Virginia) Gazette

Atlanta Journal

Fairfax (Virginia) Herald

New York Times

New York Tribune

New York World

Norfolk Virginian-Pilot

Philadelphia Daily News

Roxbury (Massachusetts) City Gazette

Washington National Tribune

Washington Star

Addresses, Articles, & Essays

Benjamin, Samuel. "We Cleared Their Way" in *Civil War Times Illustrated* 32, no. 1 (Mar./Apr. 1993): 116–17.

Cavanaugh, Lawrence, ed. "The Diary of Isaac R. Rathbun" in *New York History,* vol. 36. State Historical Association (July 1955).

Friedman, Carol Drake. "Where Did the Hero's Body Lie" in *The Historical Society of Fairfax County Virginia Yearbook, vol. 24, 1993–1994.* Fairfax: Historical Society of Fairfax, 1994.

Gardiner, William. "Incidents of Cavalry Experiences During General Pope's Campaign" in *Military Order of the Loyal Legion of the United States—Rhode Island,* vol. 34, pt. 3. Wilmington, N.C.: Broadfoot Publishing Co., 1993.

Hennessy, John J. "Thunder At Chantilly" in *North and South.* vol. 3, no. 3 (March 2000).

Henriques, Peter R., ed. "Second Manassas and the End of the War For Corporal James Tanner, USA" in *Northern Virginia Heritage,* vol. 6, no. 2, Fairfax, Va. (1984).

Hewitt, Lawrence L. "A Confederate Foreign Legion: Louisiana 'Wildcats' in the Army of Northern Virginia" in *Journal of Confederate History* 6. (1990): 53-75.

Lee, Alfred E. "From Cedar Mountain to Chantilly" in *Magazine of American History With Notes and Queries.* vol. 36. New York (December 1886).

Lochren, William. "Narrative of the First Regiment" in *Minnesota in the Civil and Indian Wars, 1861–1865,* vol. 1. St. Paul, Minn.: Pioneer Press, 1891.

Longstreet, James. "Our March Against Pope" in *The Century Magazine,* vol. 31, no. 4, New York: The Century Co. (February 1886).

Mays, Samuel Elias. "Famous Battles as a Confederate Private Saw Them" in *Tyler's Quarterly Historical and Genealogical Magazine.* vol. 4, no. 4. Richmond (April 1923).

Moore, John G. "The Battle of Chantilly" in *Military Affairs*, vol. 28, no. 2 (Summer 1964).

Morse, Charles F. "From Second Bull Run to Antietam" in *Military Order of the Loyal Legion of the United States—Missouri.* vol. 14, pt.1. Wilmington, N.C.: Broadfoot Publishing Co., 1992.

Naisawald, L. Van Loan. "A Nasty Little Battle In The Rain" in *Civil War Times Illustrated.* vol. 3, no. 3 (June 1964).

Nye, W. S. "Kearney's Death Grieved Both Sides" in *Civil War Times,* vol. 2 (January 1961).

Parker, George C. "I feel…just like writing you a letter…" in *Civil War Times Illustrated,* vol. 6, no. 1 (April 1977).

Pryor, Elizabeth Brown. "Clara Barton at Fairfax Station" in *Northern Virginia Heritage*. vol. 3, no. 2 (June 1981).

Smith, Robert R. "The Battle Of Ox Hill" in *Fairfax County and the War Between the States*. Fairfax County Civil War Centennial Commission, Fairfax, Va. (1961).

Templeman, Eleanor Lee. "Chantilly, Virginia: Historical Highlights" in *The Historical Society of Fairfax County, Virginia Yearbook, Vol. 22, 1989–1990*. Fairfax: Historical Society of Fairfax, 1990.

Thomas, Horace H. "What I Saw Under a Flag of Truce" in *Military Order of the Loyal Legion of the United States—Illinois*. vol. 10, pt. 1. Wilmington, N.C.: Broadfoot Publishing Co., 1992.

Thompson, Richard L. "Captain John Newton Ballard" in *The Historical Society of Fairfax County, Virginia Yearbook, Vol. 21, 1986–1988*. Fairfax: Historical Society of Fairfax,1988.

"Tribute To A Foe's Bravery" in *Confederate Veteran*, vol. 23, no. 12 (December 1915).

Various contributors. "Who Killed Gen. Phil Kearney?" in *Confederate Veteran*. vol. 15. no. 6 (June 1907).

Walcott, Charles F. "The Battle of Chantilly" in *Papers of the Military Historical Society of Massachusetts*. vol. 2. Boston: Military Historical Society of Massachusetts, 1895.

———. "A Revisit to the Fields of Manassas and Chantilly" in *Papers of the Military Historical Society of Massachusetts*. vol. 2. Boston: Military Historical Society of Massachusetts, 1895.

Williams, T. Harry. "The Reluctant Warrior: The Diary of N. K. Nichols" in *Civil War History*. Iowa: State University of Iowa, vol. 3, no. 1 (March 1957).

Whitehorne, Joseph W. A. "A Beastly, Comfortless Conflict: The Battle Of Chantilly" in *Blue & Gray* 4, no. 5 (May 1987): 7–23, 46–63.

Primary Sources: Letters, Diaries, Memoirs, Unit Histories

Adams, Charles R., editor. *A Post of Honor: The Pryor Letters, 1861–63*. Fort Valley, Ga.: Garret Publications, 1989.

Adams, John G. B. *Reminiscences of the 19th Massachusetts Regiment*. Boston: Wright & Potter, 1899.

Alexander, E. Porter. *Military Memoirs of a Confederate*. 1907. Reprint, New York: Da Capo Press, 1993.

Allan, William. *Stonewall Jackson, Robert E. Lee, and the Army of Northern Virginia, 1862.* New York: Da Capo Press, 1995.

Andrews, W. H. *Footprints of a Regiment: A Recollection of the First Georgia Regulars, 1861–1865.* Annotated by Richard McMurry. Atlanta: Longstreet Press, 1992.

Banes, Charles H. *History of the Philadelphia Brigade.* Philadelphia: J. P. Lippincott & Co., 1876.

Barnard, Sandy, editor. *Campaigning with the Irish Brigade: Pvt. John Ryan, 28th Massachusetts.* Terre Haute, Ind.: AST Press, 2001.

Bates, Samuel. *A Brief History of the One Hundredth Regiment (Roundheads).* New Castle, Pa.: J. C. Stevenson, 1884.

Beale, R. L. T. *History of the Ninth Virginia Cavalry.* Richmond, Va.: B. F. Johnson Publishing Co., 1899.

Beale, G. W. *A Lieutenant of Cavalry in Lee's Army.* Boston: The Gorsham Press, 1918.

Bellard, Alfred. *Gone for a Soldier: The Civil War Memoirs of Private Alfred Bellard.* Edited by Donald H. David. Boston: Little, Brown and Co., 1975.

Borcke, Heros von. *Memoirs of the Confederate War for Independence.* 1867. Reprint, Dayton, Ohio: Morningside, 1985.

Bosbyshell, Oliver C. *The 48th in the War.* Philadelphia: Avil Printing Co., 1895.

Caldwell, J. F. J. *The History of a Brigade of South Carolinians, Known First As Gregg's and Subsequently As McGowan's Brigade.* Philadelphia: King & Baird, 1866.

Casler, John O. *Four Years in the Stonewall Brigade.* 1893. Reprint, Dayton, Ohio: Morningside Press, 1971.

Cooke, John Esten. *Wearing of the Gray.* 1867. Reprint, Bloomington, Ind.: Indiana University Press, 1959.

Coward, Asbury. [Bond, Natalie & Coward, Osmun, eds.] *The South Carolinians.* New York: The Vantage Press, 1968.

Crater, Lewis. *History of the Fiftieth Regiment, Pennsylvania Veteran Volunteers, 1861–1865.* Reading, Pa.: Coleman Printing House, 1884.

Crotty, D. G. *Four Years Campaigning in the Army of the Potomac.* Grand Rapids: Dygert Brothers, 1874.

Cuffel, Charles A. *Durell's Battery in the Civil War.* Philadelphia: Craig, Finley & Co., 1900.

Davis, Charles E., Jr. *Three Years in the Army.* Boston: Estes and Lauriat, 1894.

Dawes, Rufus R. *Service with the Sixth Wisconsin Volunteers.* Dayton, Ohio: Morningside, 1984.

Denison, Frederic. *Sabres and Spurs: The First Regiment Rhode Island Cavalry.* R.I.: First Rhode Island Cavalry Veterans Association, 1876.

de Peyster, John Watts. *Personal and Military History of Philip Kearny.* New York: Rice & Gage, 1869.

Douglas, Henry Kyd. *I Rode with Stonewall.* 1940. Reprint, Chapel Hill, N.C.: University of North Carolina, 1968.

Durkin, Joseph T., editor. *Confederate Chaplain.* Milwaukee: Bruce Publishing Co., 1960.

Early, Jubal A. *Narrative of the War Between the States.* Philadelphia: Lippincott, 1912.

Eby, Cecil, Jr., editor. *A Virginia Yankee in the Civil War: The Diaries of David Hunter Strother.* Chapel Hill, N.C.: University of North Carolina, 1961.

Eisenschiml, Otto, and Ralph Newman. *Eyewitness: The Civil War as We Lived It.* New York: Grosset and Dunlap, 1956.

Floyd, Frederick C. *History of the Fortieth (Mozart) Regiment.* Boston: H. Gilson Co., 1909.

Ford, Harry E. *History of the 101st Regiment.* Syracuse: Times Publishing Co., 1898.

Fowler, Andrew L. *Memoirs of the Late Adjutant Andrew L. Fowler of the 51st N.Y.V.* New York: Ferris and Pratt, 1863.

Freeman, Douglas Southall, and Gradey McWhiney, editors. *Lee's Dispatches: Unpublished Letters of General Robert E. Lee, C.S.A. to Jefferson Davis.* New York: G. P. Putnam's, 1957.

Fulton, William Frierson. *Family Record and War Reminiscences.* N.p., Ala.: Self-published, 1914.

Gates, Theodore B. *The "Ulster Guard" [20th N.Y. State Militia] and the War of the Rebellion.* New York: Benjamin Tyrell, 1879.

Gerrish, Henry. *Letter to Lyman.* Springfield, Va.: Genealogical Books In Print, 1978.

Groat, James W. *Pages Clothed in the Plainest of Dress: The Groat Diary.* Anoka, Minn: Anoka County Historical Society, 1988.

Haupt, Herman. *Reminiscences of General Herman Haupt.* Milwaukee, Wis.: Wright & Joys, 1901.

Haynes, Draughton S. *The Field Diary of a Confederate Soldier.* Darien, Ga.: Ashantilly Press, 1963.

Hewet, Janet B., editor. *Supplement to the Official Records of the Union and Confederate Armies.* 100 vols. Wilmington, N.C.: Broadfoot Publishing Co., 1994–1996.

Hill, D. H., Jr. "North Carolina" in *Confederate Military History*, vol. 5. Edited by Clement Evans. 12 vols. Atlanta: Confederate Publishing Co., 1898.

Hotchkiss, Jedediah. *Make Me a Map of the Valley: The Civil War Journal of Stonewall Jackson's Topographer.* Dallas, Tex.: Southern Methodist University, 1973.

———. "Virginia" in *Confederate Military History,* vol. 3. Edited by Clement Evans. 12 vols. Atlanta: Confederate Publishing Co., 1898.

Houghton, W. R. and M. B. *Two Boys in the Civil War and After.* Montgomery, Ala.: The Paragon Press, 1912.

Howard, Oliver Otis. *Autobiography of Oliver Otis Howard.* 2 vols. New York: Baker and Taylor, 1907.

Huffman, James. *Ups and Downs of a Confederate Soldier.* New York: William E. Rudge's Sons, 1940.

Jackman, Lyman. *History of the Sixth New Hampshire Regiment.* Concord, N.H.: Republican Press Association, 1891.

Jackson, Mary Anna. *The Life and Letters of General Thomas J. Jackson.* New York: Harper & Bros., 1892.

Johnson, Robert U., and Clarence Buel, editors. *Battles and Leaders of the Civil War.* 4 vols. in 8 pts. 1887–1888. Reprint, Harrisburg: The Archive Society, 1991.

Johnston, Terry, editor. *"Him On One Side and Me On the Other": Civil War Letters of Alexander Campbell, 79th New York Infantry Regiment and James Campbell, 1st South Carolina Battalion.* Columbia, S.C.: University of South Carolina, 1999.

Lee, Fitzhugh. *General Lee.* 1894. Reprint, New York: Da Capo Press, 1994.

Lee, Robert E. *The Wartime Papers of R. E. Lee.* Edited by Clifford Dowdey and Louis Manarin. Boston: Little, Brown and Co., 1961.

Longstreet, James. *From Manassas to Appomattox: Memoirs of the Civil War in America.* Philadelphia: Lippincott, 1896.

Loving, Jerome M., editor. *Civil War Letters of George Washington Whitman.* Durham, N.C.: Duke University Press, 1975.

Lusk, William Thompson. *War Letters of William Thompson Lusk.* New York: Privately Printed, 1911.

Machen, Arthur W., Jr. *Letters of Arthur W. Machen with Biographical Sketch.* Baltimore: Privately Printed, 1917.

Martin, James, et al. *History of the 57th Regiment, Pennsylvania Veteran Volunteer Infantry.* 1904. Reprint, Kearny, N.J.: Belle Grove Publishing, 1985.

McClellan, George. *McClellan's Own Story.* New York: Charles Webster & Co., 1887.

McClendon, William A. *Recollections of War Times, By an Old Veteran, While under Stonewall Jackson and Lieutenant General James Longstreet; How I Got In and How I Got Out.* Montgomery, Ala.: The Paragon Press, 1909.

Mitchell, Adele H., editor. *The Letters of Major General James E. B. Stuart.* Richmond: Stuart-Mosby Historical Society, 1990.

Moore, Edward A. *The Story of a Cannoneer under Stonewall Jackson.* Lynchburg, Va.: J. P. Bell & Co., 1907.

Moore, Henry W. *"Chained to Virginia While Carolina Bleeds": Civil War Correspondence of H. W. Moore and J. W. Moore.* Walterboro, S.C.: Self-published, 1996.

Morrell, Carl A., editor. *Seymour Dexter, Union Army: Journal and Letters of Civil War Service in Co. K, 23rd New York Volunteer Infantry.* Jefferson, N.C.: McFarland & Co., 1996.

Nisbett, James Cooper. *Four Years on the Firing Line.* Chattanooga, Tenn.: The Imperial Press, 1914.

Oates, William C. *The War Between the Union and the Confederacy and Its Lost Opportunities with a History of the 15th Alabama Regiment.* New York: Neale, 1905.

Oldaker, Glenn C., compiler. *Centennial Tales: Memoirs of Colonel Chester S. Bassett French.* New York: Carlton Press, 1962.

Osborne, Seward R., editor. *The Civil War Diaries of Theodore B. Gates, 20th New York State Militia.* Hightstown, N.Y.: Longstreet House, 1991.

Owen, William Miller. *In Camp and Battle with the Washington Artillery of New Orleans.* 1885. Reprint, Louisiana: Louisiana State University Press, 1995.

Palmer, Edwin. *The Second Brigade, or Camp Life by a Volunteer.* Montpelier, Vt.: Self-published, 1864.

Parker, Thomas H. *History of the 51st Regiment of Pennsylvania Volunteers.* Philadelphia: King & Baird, 1869.

Pender, William Dorsey. *One of Lee's Best Men: The Civil War Letters of General William Dorsey Pender.* Edited by William Hassler. Chapel Hill, N.C.: University of North Carolina, 1995.

Preston, Noble D. *History of the Tenth Regiment of Cavalry New York State Volunteers.* New York: D. Appleton & Co., 1892.

Priest, John Michael. *From New Bern to Fredericksburg: Captain James Wren's Diary.* Shippensburg, Pa.: White Mane Publishing, 1990.

Pyne, Henry R. *Ride to War: History of the First New Jersey Cavalry.* New Brunswick, N.J.: Rutgers University Press, 1961.

Rhodes, Elisha Hunt. *All for the Union: Civil War Diary and Letters of Elisha Hunt Rhodes, 2nd Rhode Island.* New York: Orion, 1985.

Ropes, John Codman. "The Army Under Pope" in *Campaigns of the Civil War.* vol. 4, New York: Charles Scribners Sons, 1882.

Rosenblatt, Emil, and Ruth Rosenblatt, editors. *Hard Marching Every Day: The Civil War Letters of Private Wilbur Fisk.* Lawrence, Kans.: University Press of Kansas, 1992.

Sauers, Richard, editor. *The Civil War Journal of Colonel William J. Bolton, 51st Pennsylvania.* Conshohocken, Pa.: Combined Publishing, 2000.

Schaff, Morris. *The Battle of the Wilderness.* New York: Houghton Mifflin, 1910.

Sears, Stephen, editor. *The Civil War Papers of George B. McClellan: Selected Correspondence 1860–1865.* New York: Ticknor & Fields, 1989.

———. *For Country Cause and Leader: The Civil War Journal of Charles B. Hayden.* New York: Ticknor & Fields, 1993.

———. *On Campaign with the Army of the Potomac: The Civil War Journal of Theodore Ayrault Dodge.* New York: Cooper Square Press, 2001.

Shoemaker, J. J. *Shoemaker's Battery, Stuart Horse Artillery, Pelham's Battalion.* 1908. Reprint, Gaithersburg, Md.: Butternut & Blue, 1994.

Sneden, Robert Knox. *Eye of the Storm: A Civil War Odyssey.* New York: The Free Press, 2000.

Sorrell, G. Moxley. *Recollections of a Confederate Staff Officer.* 1905. Reprint, New York: Smithmark, 1994.

Southern Historical Society. *Southern Historical Society Papers.* 52 vols. Richmond, Va.: Self-published, 1876–1959.

Sparks, David S., editor. *Inside Lincoln's Army: The Diary of Marsena Rudolph Patrick, Provost Marshal General, Army of the Potomac.* New York: Thomas Yoseloff, 1964.

Stearns, Austin C. *Three Years with Company K.* Rutherford, N.J.: Fairleigh Dickinson University Press, 1976.

Stepp, John W., and William I. Hill, editors. *Mirror of War: The Washing Star Reports the Civil War.* Englewood, N.J.: Prentice Hall, 1961.

Stevens, Hazard. *The Life of Isaac Ingalls Stevens.* 2 vols. Boston: Houghton Mifflin & Co., 1900.

Stone, James Madison. *Personal Recollections of the Civil War.* Boston: Self-Published, 1918.

Styple, William B., editor. *Letters from the Peninsula: The Civil War Letters of General Philip Kearny.* Kearny, N.J.: Belle Grove Pub., 1988.

———. *Writing and Fighting the Civil War: Soldier Correspondence to the New York Sunday Mercury.* Kearny, N.J.: Belle Grove Publishing, 2000.

Tanner, W. S., Sr. *Reminiscences of the War Between the States.* Cowpens, S.C.: Privately Printed, 1931.

Tapert, Annette, editor. *The Brothers' War: Civil War Letters to Their Loved Ones from the Blue and the Gray.* New York: Times Books, 1988.

Taylor, Walter H. *General Lee: His Campaigns in Virginia, 1861– 1865, With Personal Reminiscences.* 1906. Reprint, Dayton, Ohio: Morningside, 1975.

Thacker, Victor, editor. *French Harding: Civil War Memoirs.* Parsons, W.Va.: McClain Printing Co., 2000.

Thomas, Henry W. *History of the Doles-Cook Brigade.* 1903. Reprint, Dayton, Ohio: Morningside, 1981.

Todd, William. *The 79th Highlanders.* New York: Brandow, Barton and Co., 1886.

United Daughters of the Confederacy: Georgia Division. *Confederate Reminiscences and Letters 1861–1865.* vol. 1. N.p., Ga.: Self-published, 1995.

United Daughters of the Confederacy: South Carolina Division. *Recollections and Reminiscences 1861–1865.* vol. 1. N.p., S.C.: Self-published, 1990.

Waitt, Ernest Linden, compiler. *History of the 19th Regiment, Massachusetts Volunteer Infantry.* Salem, Mass.: The Salem Press, 1906.

Walcott, Charles F. *History of the Twenty-First Regiment Massachusetts Volunteers.* Boston: Houghton Mifflin, 1882.

Welch, Spencer Glasgow. *A Confederate Surgeon's Letters to His Wife.* 1911. Reprint, Marietta, Ga.: Continental Book Co., 1954.

Weld, Stephen. *War Diary and Letters of Stephen Minot Weld.* 2nd ed. Mass.: Massachusetts Historical Society, 1979.

Whitman, William E. S., and Charles H. True, *Maine in the War for the Union.* Lewiston, Maine: Nelson Dingley & Co., 1865.

Wise, George. *History of the 17th Virginia Infantry. C.S.A.* Baltimore: Kelly, Piet & Co., 1870.

———. *Campaigns and Battles of the Army of Northern Virginia.* New York: Neale Co., 1916.

Woodward, E. M. *Our Campaigns: The Second Regiment Pennsylvania Reserve Volunteers.* Shippensburg, Pa.: Burd Street Press, 1995.

Worsham, John H. *One of Jackson's Foot Cavalry.* New York: Neale Publishing Co., 1912.

Wright, James A. *No More Gallant a Deed: A Civil War Memoir of the First Minnesota Volunteers.* St. Paul, Minn.: Minnesota Historical Society Press, 2001.

Secondary Sources

Andrews, J. Cutler. *The North Reports the Civil War.* Pa.: University of Pittsburgh Press, 1955.

Armstrong, Richard L. *25th Virginia Infantry and 9th Battalion Virginia Infantry.* Lynchburg, Va.: H. E. Howard, 1990.

Barton, William E. *The Life of Clara Barton.* Boston: Houghton Mifflin Co., 1922.

Blair, William. *Virginia's Private War: Feeding Body and Soul in the Confederacy, 1861–1865.* New York: Oxford University Press, 1998.

Boge, Georgie, and Margie Holder. *Paving over the Past.* Washington D.C.: Island Press, 1993.

Conservation Fund, The. [Kennedy, Frances H., editor and principal contributor] *The Civil War Battlefield Guide.* New York: Houghton Mifflin Co., 1998.

Cooling, B. Franklin. *Symbol, Sword, and Shield: Defending Washington during the Civil War.* Hamden, Conn.: Archon Books, 1975.

Cozzens, Peter. *General John Pope: A Life for the Nation.* Urbana, Ill.: University of Illinois Press, 2000.

Dalton, Peter P. *With Our Faces to the Foe: A History of the 4th Maine Infantry in the War of the Rebellion.* Union, Maine: Union Publishing Co., 1998.

Davis, Oliver. *Life of David Bell Birney, Major General, United States Volunteers.* Philadelphia: King & Baird, 1867.

Dornbusch, C. E., compiler. *Military Bibliography of the Civil War.* 4 vols. New York: New York Public Library, 1989.

Dunn, Craig L. *Harvestfields of Death: The Twentieth Indiana Volunteers of Gettysburg.* Carmel, Ind.: Guild Press, 1999.

Evans, D'Anne. *The Story of Oakton, Virginia: 1758–1982.* Oakton, Va.: Greater Oakton Citizens Association, 1982.

Freeman, Douglas Southall. *Lee's Lieutenants: A Study in Command.* 3 vols. New York: Scribners, 1942–1944.

———. *R. E. Lee: A Biography.* 4 vols. New York: Charles Scribners Sons, 1934–1940.

Gaff, Alan. *Brave Men's Tears: The Iron Brigade at Brawner's Farm.* Dayton, Ohio: Morningside, 1985.

Gamble, Robert S. *Sully: The Biography of a House.* Chantilly, Va.: Sully Foundation Ltd., 1973.

Gannon, James P. *Irish Rebels, Confederate Tigers: A History of the 6th Louisiana Volunteers, 1861–1865.* Campbell, Calif.: Savas, 1998.

Gavin, William Gilfillan. *Campaigning with the Roundheads: A History of the 100th Pennsylvania Volunteer Infantry Regiment in the American Civil War 1861–1865.* Dayton, Ohio: Morningside, 1989.

Hale, Laura V., and Stanley S. Phillips. *History of the Forty-Ninth Virginia Infantry, C.S.A.* Virginia: published by the authors, 1981.

Harris, Brayton. *Blue and Gray in Black and White: Newspapers in the Civil War.* Washington D.C.: Brassey's, 1999.

Hassler, William Woods. *A. P. Hill: Lee's Forgotten General.* Chapel Hill, N.C.: University of North Carolina, 1962.

Hennessy, John J. *Return to Bull Run: The Campaign and Battle of Second Manassas.* New York: Simon and Schuster, 1993.

Imlay, John, et al. *The Oakley Site 44FX734.* Archeological Society of Virginia, Northern Virginia Chapter. Occasional Paper 86-2. November, 1986.

Jones, Terry. *Lee's Tigers: The Louisiana Infantry in the Army of Northern Virginia.* Baton Rouge, La.: Louisiana State University, 1987.

Kearny, Thomas. *General Philip Kearny: Battle Soldier of Five Wars.* New York: G. P. Putnam's Sons, 1937.

Kinsley, Ardyce. *The Fitzhugh Lee Sampler.* N.p., Privately Printed, 1990.

Krick, Robert K. *Lee's Colonels: A Biographical Register of the Field Officers of the Army of Northern Virginia.* Dayton, Ohio: Morningside, 1979.

Leech, Margaret. *Reveille in Washington 1860–1865.* New York: Harper and Row, 1941.

Lord, Francis A. *Lincoln's Railroad Man: Herman Haupt.* Rutherford, N.J.: Fairleigh Dickinson University Press, 1969.

Maxwell, William Quentin. *Lincoln's Fifth Wheel: The Political History of the United States Sanitary Commission.* New York: Longmans, Green and Co., 1956.

McConnell, William F. *Remember Reno: A Biography of Major General Jesse L. Reno.* Shippensburg, Pa.: White Mane, 1996.

McKnight, William Mark. *Blue Bonnets O'er the Border: The 79th New York Cameron Highlanders.* Shippensburg, Pa.: White Mane, 1998.

Miller, Francis T. *The Photographic History of the Civil War.* 10 vols. New York: The Review of Reviews Co., 1911.

Mottelay, Paul F., and T. Campbell-Copeland, editors. *The Soldier in Our Civil War: A Pictorial History of the Conflict, 1861–1865.* 2 vols. Richmond and New York: Stanley Bradley Publishing Co., 1890.

Netherton, N.; Rose, R.; Meyer, D.; Wagner, P.; DiVincenzo, M. *Fairfax, Virginia: A City Traveling through Time.* Fairfax: History of Fairfax Round Table, 1997.

Oates, Stephen. *Clara Barton: A Woman of Valor.* New York: The Free Press, 1994.

Osborne, Charles. *Jubal: The Life and Times of General Jubal A. Early, CSA.* Chapel Hill, N.C.: Algonquin Books of Chapel Hill, 1992.

Palmer, Michael. *Lee Moves North: Robert E. Lee on the Offensive.* New York: John Wiley & Sons, 1998.

Pryor, Elizabeth Brown. *Walney: Two Centuries of a Northern Virginia Plantation.* Fairfax: Fairfax County Office of History and Archeology, 1984.

Richards, Kent. *Isaac I. Stevens: Young Man in a Hurry.* Pullman, Wash.: Washington State University Press, 1993.

Robertson, James I., Jr. *Stonewall Jackson.* New York: Macmillan, 1997.

Schutz, Wallace J., and Walter N. Trenerry. *Abandoned by Lincoln: A Military Biography of John Pope.* Chicago: University of Illinois Press, 1990.

Sibley, F. Ray, Jr. *The Confederate Order of Battle, Volume 1: The Army of Northern Virginia.* Shippensburg, Pa.: White Mane, 1996.

Smith, Eugenia B. *Centreville, Virginia: Its History and Architecture.* Fairfax: Fairfax County Office of Planning, 1973.

Stackpole, Edward. *From Cedar Mountain to Antietam.* Harrisburg, Pa.: Stackpole, 1959.

Sutherland, Daniel E. *The Emergence of Total War.* Fort Worth, Tex.: Ryan Place Publishers, 1996.

Warner, Ezra J. *Generals in Blue.* Baton Rouge: Louisiana State University Press, 1964.

————. *Generals in Gray*. Baton Rouge: Louisiana State University Press, 1964.

Wellman, Manley Wade. *Giant in Gray: A Biography of Wade Hampton*. New York: Charles Scribner's Sons, 1949.

Wert, Jeffry. *A Brotherhood of Valor*. New York: Simon & Schuster, 1999.

White, Gregory C. *This Most Bloody and Cruel Drama: A History of the 31st Georgia Infantry*. Baltimore, Md.: Butternut and Blue, 1997.

Internet

The 15 Most Underrated Battles of the Civil War. Civil War Interactive; available from World Wide Web @ http://205.247.235.71/urmain1.htm

Letters of the Civil War: A Compilation of Letters, Stories, Diaries from the Soldiers, Sailors, Nurses, Politicians, Ministers, Journalists and Citizens during the War of the Rebellion from the Newspapers of Massachusetts; available from World Wide Web @ http://www.letterscivilwar.com/

McConahy, Tami. *Civil War Era Newspaper Scrapbook, New Castle "Courant" Articles*. Brown, Reverend Robert A. Letters; available from World Wide Web @ http://members.aol.com/dwelchk2/100thscrap.html

INDEX

References to illustrations are printed in boldface type.

A

Alabama troops
  15th, 36, 56, 64
Alexander, E. Porter, 110
Alexandria, Va., 108, 120
Anderson, Tige, 90
Archer, James A., 8, 72, 78
Arlington Heights, 98
Army of the Potomac, 9, 122
Army of Virginia, 122
Artillery, Confederate
  lack of at Ox Hill, 72

B

Ballard, John N., 126, **127**
Banks, Nathaniel, 3, 7, 17
Barlow, Maria, 108
Barton, Clara, 102–4
Bayard, George, 38, 46
Beale, George, 86
Behan, William, 94
Belcher, Horatio, 58, 61, 110
Bellard, Alfred, 111
Benham, Henry, 131
Benjamin, Samuel, 56
Birney, David, 59, 77, 82, **82**, 90, 134
Bracken, Elisha, 11
Branch, Lawrence O'Bryan, 8, 53, **53**, 78
Bristoe Station, Va., 10
Brockenbrough, John M., 53, **53**
Brown, Reverend Robert F., 82
Brown, William F., 65, **65**
Bull Run, 17
Burial of soldiers, 19–20, 22, 107

C

Casualties
  abandoned on the field, 105–6
  treatment of, 101–3
Cavalry, Union
  fatigue of, 23–24
Cedar Mountain
  battle of, 6–9
Centreville, Va., 17, 32
Chain Bridge, 113
Chantilly
  description of, 24–25
  estate of, 1, 86
Chantilly battlefield, **57**
Chase, Salmon P., 122
Chinn Ridge, 14
Christ, Benjamin, 63
Civilians
  effects of war on, 107–8
Clark, William, 88
Colston, William, 65
Coward, Asbury, 17
Cox, Jacob, 121
Crawford, Samuel, 7
Cub Run, 19, 22–23, 48
Cutter, Dr. Calvin, 105

D

Dana, Napoleon, 113
Davis, Jefferson, 117, 119
Dodge, Theodore, 89
Douglas, Marcellus, 64
Dranesville, Va., 27
Durell, George, 52, 72, 75

E

Early, Jubal A., 63, 66, **68**, 72, 84
Early, Sam, 67
Elias, Samuel, 112
Enfield rifle
  problems with, 88

F

Fairfax County
  effects of war on, 108
Fairfax Court House, Va., 108
  village of, 115
Fairfax Station, 103
Farinholt, Benjamin, 95
Ferrero, Edward, 51, **51**, 72
Field, Charles, 52
Fisk, Wilbur, 16
Flint Hill
  skirmish at, 111–15
Flint Hill, Va., 45
Food, lack of, 38
Forno, Henry, 63
Franklin, William, 30
Fremont, John, 3
Frying Pan Church, 39

G

Gardiner, William, 86
Georgia troops
  1st, 90
  12th, 65, 69
  49th, 83, 84
Germantown, Va., 26, 33
  Federal reinforcing at, 40–42, 109–10
Gerrish, Henry, 15
Gorman, Willis, 113
Graham, William, 59
Graves, Charles, 83
Gregg, Maxcy, 38, 71, **71**
Groat, James, 115
Groveton, 13
Grover, Cuvier, 59
Gum Springs Road, 22, 35

H

Halleck, Henry, 1, 36, 123
Hammond, William, 106
Hampton, Wade, 112
Haupt, Herman, 104, 106
Haymarket, Va., 107
Heintzelman, Samuel, 42, 48, 59
Henry House Hill, 14
Hight, Thomas, 26, 33
Hill, Ambrose P., 13, 22, **23**, 36, 52, 54, 78, 86

Hill, D. H., 18, 119
Hinks, Edward, 41
Hooker, Joseph, 32, 42–43, 59, 86, 134
Hotchkiss, Jedediah, 16, 39, 117, **117**
Howard, Oliver O., 33, 112, 133
Hunter, Alexander, 111

I

Indiana troops
  20th, 59

J

Jackson, Thomas J., 3, 7, 9, 18, 33, 35, **39**, 44, 70, 86, 89, 91, 119
Johnson, Bradley T., 38
Journalists
  censorship of, 1–2

K

Kearny, Philip, 13, 58–59, 75, 78, **79**, 82–83
  death of, 83–87
  prewar biog., 132–33
Kearny Patch, 134–35
Kearny-Stevens Monuments, 126, **129**
King, Rufus, 12
Knight, William, 107, 108

L

Lawton, Alexander R., 36, 54, 64, 69, 80, **80**
Lee, Fitzhugh, 22, 26, 43
Lee, Robert E., 6, 17, 26, 86, 91, 109, 116, 117, 118–19, 123
Leesburg, Va., 119
Lincoln, Abraham, 3, 122–23
Little River Turnpike, 22, 32, 35, 70
  description of, 36–37
Longstreet, James, 14, 18, 22, 34, 38, 90, **90**, 91, 119
Louisiana troops
  1st, 86
  6th, 63
  14th, 69
Lusk, William, 56, 82

M

Machen, Emma, 25
Magruder, John, 107
Maguire, Dr. Hunter, 89
Maine troops
  3rd, 77, 80
  4th, 77, 80, 86
Manassas Station, 11
Maryland troops (Union)
  2nd, 51

Massachusetts troops
  19th, 41, 113–15
  20th, 41
  21st, 72–75, 83, 86, 87, 88, 102–3
  28th, 52, 61, 69
McClellan, George, 6, 13, 31, 41, 46, 120, 121
  feelings toward John Pope, 122–23
McClendon, William, 36
McDowell, Irvin, 3, 12, 15, 42, 44, 48, 121
McGinnis, Edward, 86
Meade, George, 27
medical supplies
  lack of, 31, 105–7
Michigan troops
  2nd, 90, 98
  3rd, 90
  5th, 90
  7th, 41
  8th, 52, 61
Milan house, 49, 56
Minnesota troops
  1st, 113–15
Monoghan, William, 63, 64
Moore, Edward, 21

N

Nagle, James, 51, 76
New Hampshire troops
  6th, 51, 76
  9th, 51
New Jersey troops
  1st, 27
  3rd, 27
New York troops
  1st, 77
  10th Cavalry, 27
  37th, 90
  38th, 77
  40th, 60, 77
  42nd, 41
  46th, 52
  51st, 72–75
  79th, 49, **49**, 52, 56, 58, 60–61, 63, 69, 82, 93, 130, 131
  80th, 43
  86th, 118
  101st, 77
North Carolina troops
  16th, 71, 78
  18th, 78
  34th, 71, 78

O

Oates, William, 64
Orange & Alexandria Railroad, 6

Orr, James, 9, 11
Ox Hill, 16
  casualties at, 100
  post-battle conditions, 94–96
  weather conditions during battle, 70
Ox Hill, vs. Chantilly as proper name of the battle, 16
Ox Hill Battlefield Park, 125–28

P

Parker, George, 88
Parker, Thomas, 95
Parole system, 117–18
Patrick, Marsena, 43
Pelham, John, 23, 43
Pender, William Dorsey, 8, 71, 110, **110**
Pennsylvania troops
  Durell's battery, 75–76, 98
  1st Cavalry, 27
  48th, 51, 76, 77
  50th, 52, 63, 76
  51st, 32, 72, 76, 92, 98
  57th, 78, 87
  63rd, 59
  99th, 90
  100th, 52, 58, 82
  105th, 59
Philadelphia Brigade, 33
Pickett, George, 47
Pleasant Valley, 34
Poe, Orlando, 59, 80, 90, 95, **97**, 121
Point of Rocks, Md., 119
Pope, John, 1, **4**, 15, 30–32, 41–42, 44, 120
  arrival as new commander, 3–6
  dismissal from command, 122
  general orders of, 5–6
Porter, Fitz-John, 14, 31, 46
Port Republic
  battle of, 63
Potomac River, 119
Prisoners of war
  parole and treatment of, 117–18
Pryor, Roger, 19

R

Rappahannock River, 9
Rathbun, Isaac, 118
Reid house, 49, 54, 93
Reno, Jesse, 19, 47, **47**, 51–52, 60, 72, 93, 106
Reynolds, John (Union General), 48
Reynolds, John (19th Massachusetts), 114
Rhode Island troops
  Randolph's battery, 78

1st Cavalry, 43
2nd, 44
Rice, Nicholas, 19, 52, 58
Ricketts, James B., 44
Ring, George, 63
Robertson, Beverly H., 22, 26
Robinson, John C., 59, 95, **98**

S

Secessionville
 battle of, 131
Second Manassas
 battle of, 12–15
Seibert, John, 92
Seven Pines
 battle of, 82
Simmons, Charles, 104
Smith, "Extra Billy," 40
Smith, James L., 45–46
Snakenberg, William, 9, 69
Sneden, Robert, 16
South Carolina troops
 1st, 72
 12th, 71
 13th, 71
 14th, 71
St. Mary's Church, 103
Stanton, Edwin, 106, 122
Starke, William E., 36, 38, 67, **67**, 72
Stevens, Hazard, 56, 58
Stevens, Isaac, 47–48, 51, **61**
 burial of, 93
 charge of his division at Ox Hill, 54–72
 death of, 63
 prewar biog. of, 130–31
Stewart, Charles
 farm of, 71
Stone, James, 86
Stringfellow Road, 26, 38
Strong, Henry B., 54, 58, 63, 64
Stuart, Charles Calvin, 24, 107
Stuart, James E. B. (Jeb), 22–23, 26, **29**,
  30, 39, 40, 44–45, 112, 114
Sudley Ford, 22, 34, 39

Sudley Springs, 12
Sumner, Edwin, 33, 49, 112

T

Taylor, Walter, 86
Thomas, Edward L., 71, **71**
Thoroughfare Gap, 10
Toombs, Robert, 90
Torbert, Alfred, 41
Trimble, Isaac, 56, 65

U

U.S. troops
 2nd Cavalry, 26

V

Vermont troops
 12th, 107
Vienna, Va., 113, 115
Virginia troops
 2nd, 65
 9th Cavalry, 27, 86
 12th Cavalry, 27
 13th, 65, 66
 21st, 38
 25th, 66
 31st, 66, 84
 40th, 54
 49th, 40
 57th, 107
von Borcke, Heros, 27, 45, 113

W

Walcott, Charles, 74, 87
Walker, James, 65
Walney, 25
Walney Road, 26
Warrenton Turnpike, 12, 27, 39, 59, 98
Washington Star, 120
Welch, Spencer, 101
Welles, Gideon, 120
White's Ford, 119
Whiteside, John, 123
Winder, Charles, 8
Witcher, William, 38

We Shall Meet Again
The First Battle of Manassas (Bull Run), July 18-21, 1861
JoAnna M. McDonald

The boys of 1861 donned clean, new uniforms, picked up their muskets, and marched to war singing and laughing. On July 16, 1861, the Union army, commanded by Brigadier General Irvin McDowell, moved out of Washington, D.C. and Alexandria, Virginia, toward Manassas Junction, only 26 miles southwest of the capital. Confederate General P. G. T. Beauregard deployed his army along the west bank of a small creek called Bull Run.

On that hot, humid Sunday, July 21, at 6:00 a.m. someone fired the first shot of the first large-scale battle of the American Civil War. Nearly 30,000 soldiers received their baptism by fire during those 10 1/2 hours. Their courage was tested, and brigades and individuals received reputations which followed them into history. This was the place where the famous rebel yell was born.

ISBN 1-57249-108-6
6" x 9", 244 Pages
HC $27.95

Approximately 878 Union and Confederate soldiers were killed that day and another 2,489 were wounded. Afterwards, the Confederates, wearied from the day's fighting, either collapsed and slept or looked for a fallen comrade. Private John Casler, 33rd Virginia, found his best friend dead, shot through the heart. Casler, overcome with grief, recalled, "Al sat down by him and took a hearty cry, and then thinks I, 'It does not look well for a soldier to cry,' but I could not help it." As Private Berrien Zettler, 8th Georgia, walked among the mutilated bodies, he thought to himself, "Surely, surely, there will never be another battle...I felt sure there would never be another."

A journalist from the *London Daily News*, however, predicted, "The grand controversy between the North and the South has at length reached the point it has been for years past gradually approaching—the ultima ratio of force; and the sword having now been drawn in earnest, it must be fought out."

About the Author

Author of several battlefield guides, including The World Will Long Remember: A Guide to the Battle of Gettysburg; Goodbye Boys! Goodbye!: A Guide to the High Water Mark, July 2–3, 1863; *and* Give them the Bayonet: A Guide to the Battle for Henry Hill, July 21, 1861, *JoAnna M. McDonald has been a student of military history for sixteen years. She again shares her research and photographic work in her in-depth look at the First Battle of Manassas.*

We Shall Meet Again: The First Battle of Manassas (Bull Run), July 18–21, 1861, *is the first book on this subject to include forty-five maps and over 200 photographs of the individual soldiers.*

Rocks and War
Geology and the Civil War Campaign of Second Manassas
E-An Zen and Alta Walker

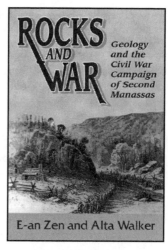

Here is the first study of the Battle of Second Manassas to show the importance of the landscape through which the opposing generals maneuvered. Stonewall Jackson's, James Longstreet's, and Robert E. Lee's understanding of those landforms decisively tilted the campaign's outcome in their favor. Their activities took place through four different geologic formations. But this started with John Pope's use of the Rappahannock and Rapidan Rivers as defensive positions. At the same time the Blue Ridge and the Bull Run Mountain shielded most of the Confederates.

Longstreet and Lee had to move through Thoroughfare Gap to join Jackson and attack Pope. That gap, carved through the resistant quartzite of Bull Run Mountain by Broad Run's waters, is a focal point of this account.

Jackson, after a daring raid on the large supply depot at Manassas Junction, went behind a railroad embankment below Stony Ridge to wait for the rest of Lee's Army. To reach Jackson, Longstreet had to pass through the gap. They were able to move through it easily because of Pope's failure to understand its strategic importance and to defend it. They then fought the climactic Battle of Second Manassas in an area of flat-topped, open ridges dissected by steep ravines known as the Culpeper Basin. Those same ravines slowed the Confederates and allowed the Federals to escape.

ISBN: 1-57249-197-3
6" x 9", 116 Pages
PB $9.95

About the Authors
E-An Zen

A former president of the Geological Society of America, Dr. Zen is also a member of the National Academy of Sciences. He has long been involved in programs bringing geological knowledge to the lay public.

Alta Walker

A specialist in military geology, currently with the U.S. Army Corps of Engineers, Dr. Walker is a published free-lance writer.

Rocks and War *is a study of the interplay between warfare and terrain. Taking this book onto the battlefield, or using it in conjunction with the standard histories, readers of this book will gain a new way of interpreting Civil War battles.*

Nowhere to Run
The Wilderness, May 4th & 5th, 1864 (Volume 1)
John Michael Priest

When the armies entered the Wilderness, they were changed forever. Within thirty-six hours after the Army of the Potomac began its attempt to flank the Army of Northern Virginia and attack Richmond, the armies became locked in combat. In two days of bloody fighting by disconnected and often confused but heroic forces, Lee fought Grant to a tactical draw at a cost of approximately 18,000 Union and an estimated 8,000 Confederate casualties.

Only John Michael Priest could capture the human impact of that fighting, action that exhausted both armies as they fought towards Cold Harbor. This first of two volumes brings the reader to the evening of May 5, 1864.

ISBN 0-942597-74-5
6" x 9", 336 Pages
HC $29.95

Features forty-five carefully drawn two-color maps and extensive notes.

Victory Without Triumph
The Wilderness, May 6th & 7th, 1864 (Volume 2)
John Michael Priest

Brigadier General John Gregg spurred around to the front of his regiments. Turning his horse to face the line, he shouted, "General Lee wants us to go and drive those people out. Remember, Hood's Brigade, that General Lee's eyes are upon you and his heart is with you. Forward!"....When the veterans stepped off, Lee removed his hat and, standing in the stirrups, exclaimed loudly, as if to reassure himself, "Texans always move them." The Texans who heard him responded with a tremendous rebel yell. His mere presence electrified the line.... Tears of pride streamed down Private Leonard G. Gee's face. The orderly, who was screaming and yipping at the top of his lungs, choked back his tears and cried, "I would charge into hell for that old man."

ISBN 1-57249-009-8
6" x 9", 352 Pages
HC $34.95

Charge into that same hell from the perspective of the officers and enlisted men who lived through it in *Victory Without Triumph*, the second of John Michael Priest's volumes on the Battle of the Wilderness. Priest meticulously details the vicious infantry fighting along the Pack Road, Longstreet's counterstrike against the II Corps, the cavalry operations of both armies near Todd's Tavern, and John B. Gordon's daring assault against the Army of the Potomac's right flank. Embellished with 38 detailed, two-colored maps, follow the Army of the Potomac and the Army of Northern Virginia through the last two days of the campaign which signaled the advent of Ulysses S. Grant into the Eastern theater of the war.

Features thirty-eight carefully drawn two-color detailed maps from the regimental level and extensive notes. Over 80 photos and maps complement the text.

About the Author
John Michael Priest is the author of the highly acclaimed *Antietam: The Soldiers' Battle, Before Antietam: The Battle for South Mountain* and other works.